The Workplace

The Workplace
CHART YOUR CAREER

Dr. Joe Pace

Boston   Burr Ridge, IL   Dubuque, IA   Madison, WI   New York   San Francisco   St. Louis
Bangkok   Bogotá   Caracas   Kuala Lumpur   Lisbon   London   Madrid   Mexico City
Milan   Montreal   New Delhi   Santiago   Seoul   Singapore   Sydney   Taipei   Toronto

Higher Education

*A division of the **McGraw-Hill** Companies*

THE PROFESSIONAL DEVELOPMENT SERIES: BOOK 4: THE WORKPLACE: CHART YOUR CAREER
Published by McGraw-Hill, a business unit of The McGraw-Hill Companies, Inc., 1221 Avenue of the Americas, New York, NY, 10020.
Copyright © 2006 by The McGraw-Hill Companies, Inc. All rights reserved. No part of this publication may be reproduced or
distributed in any form or by any means, or stored in a database or retrieval system, without the prior written consent of The McGraw-
Hill Companies, Inc., including, but not limited to, in any network or other electronic storage or transmission, or broadcast for distance
learning.

Some ancillaries, including electronic and print components, may not be available to customers outside the United States.

This book is printed on acid-free paper.

7 8 9 0 CUS/CUS 15 14 13 12 11

ISBN: 978-0-07-829831-8
MHID: 0-07-829831-8

Editor in Chief: *Emily Barrosse*
Publisher: *Beth Mejia*
Executive Editor: *David S. Patterson*
Developmental Editor: *Anne Sachs*
Senior Marketing Manager: *Leslie Oberhuber*
Managing Editor: *Jean Dal Porto*
Project Manager: *Jean R. Starr*
Art Director: *Jeanne Schreiber*
Associate Designer: *Srdjan Savanovic*
Text Designer: *Kiera Pohl*
Cover Designer: *Srdjan Savanovic*
Illustrator(s): *Ayelet Arbel*
Photo Research Coordinator: *Natalia C. Peschiera*
Associate Art Editor: *Ayelet Arbel*
Cover Credit: © Keith Brofsky/Getty Images
Media Producer: *Todd Vaccaro*
Supplements Director: *Nadia Bidwell*
Production Supervisor: *Janean A. Utley*
Composition: *9.5/12 Palatino by Carlisle Communications, Ltd.*
Printing: *PMS Black, 45# New Era Matte, Von Hoffmann/Custom*

The Internet addresses listed in the text were accurate at the time of publication. The inclusion of a website does not indicate an
endorsement by the authors of McGraw-Hill, and McGraw-Hill does not guarantee the accuracy of the information presented at
these sites.

www.mhhe.com

Contents

As a psychologist and former college president involved in higher education for over 36 years, I have often been asked what skills most directly contribute to career success.

The questioner generally expects me to talk about job skills. Thirty years ago, it would have been typing. Today, it might be familiarity with common workplace software.

But the fact is that most employers don't care how fast you type or how well you align columns on a spreadsheet.

What Do Employers Want?

In a recent survey[1], business owners and corporate executives in the United States were asked to rate what they valued most in a new employee:

- Dependability—35%
- Honesty—27%
- Good Attitude—19%
- Competence—19%

What does this tell us? It says, simply, that 81 percent of corporations in the United States rate the personal qualities of dependability, honesty and attitude—what I call *professionalism*—above any skills-based competencies.

The Need for *Professionalism*

Does it make sense that employers value professionalism over what we generally think of as job-related skills? Certainly. All jobs and businesses are different. Even companies manufacturing similar products in the same city will have their own unique procedures and policies. Working for one does not mean you can easily transition into working for another. Employers know

---

[1]*Padgett Business Services* quarterly survey of service and retail clients.

this. They know that they will have to train you in the skills necessary for your job and they are willing to do this. What employers want from you are the internal qualities that make you trainable.

Employers want you to be reliable; they want you to be hardworking; and they want you to be ethical. In a word, employers look for the qualities that make a person *professional*.

Why *The Professional Development Series?*

The sad fact is that most colleges and schools spend an overwhelming majority of time and energy developing hard skills while ignoring the personal qualities of character and dependability that actually get people hired. The good news is that—like typing or programming—professionalism can be taught.

My aim in developing this *Professional Development Series* has been to teach the personal skills that lead to job and career success. The *Series* is based both on my own research on career success and my experience as a lecturer, college president, and mentor. The material I present in the *Series* is the same material I have used to guide thousands of students and to train hundreds of instructors across North America. The goal for teachers who use the *Series* is to help turn out graduates ready to meet the challenges of the fast-paced professional world. The goal for students learning with the *Series* is to succeed in their chosen careers and, more importantly, to succeed in life.

The Books in *The Professional Development Series*

The Professional Development Series is easy to read and user-friendly. The books are brief, because you are busy. The books are practical, because you need specific guidance, not vague assurances. Each book and every chapter uses a consistent organization of text and features to structure the material.

Book 1: *The Workplace:* **Today and Tomorrow**

Book One is an orientation to the world of work. In it, you will consider the occupations that are most likely to have job openings in the coming years, how to prepare yourself to fill these openings, and what the workplace environment is like in the 21stcentury. Professional business protocol, professional presence, and a customer-first attitude are also explored and discussed.

Book 2: *The Workplace:* **Interpersonal Strengths and Leadership**

Professional success in the twenty-first century demands that people work together to achieve their goals. Book Two: *Interpersonal Strengths and Leadership*, explores and develops the skills that make a person a good teammate and a good leader. Developing a standard of excellence and pride in your work along with understanding ethics, trust and respect are also covered. Thinking strategically and modeling leadership techniques are addressed as well.

Book 3: *The Workplace:* **Personal Skills for Success**

Time management and stress management come to mind when we talk about *Personal Skills for Success* and in Book 3, you will develop and practice these skills. You will also be encouraged to think about who you are and what you believe and to use what you learn to establish goals for the future and to develop a plan to achieve those goals. Communicating, presenting ideas and concepts as well as thinking critically and creatively are also covered.

Book 4: *The Workplace:* **Chart Your Career**

One day you leave school and you have a job; twenty years later you look back and realize that you have a career. How can you make sure that the career you have is fulfilling and rewarding? How

can you avoid or overcome the inevitable missteps—taking the wrong job, for example—and get your career back on track? Book 4 offers guidance on planning a career and, more importantly, on developing, changing, and maintaining it.

Features of Each Book in *The Professional Development Series*

Every chapter of each book has a consistent format, clearly organizing the material to help you learn.

Beginning Each Chapter

What Will You Do?: The entire plan for the chapter is set out in *What Will You Do?*. Each section within the chapter is called out with a one-sentence summary describing the content.

Why Do You Need to Know This?: The information in each chapter is there for a reason. *Why Do You Need to Know This?* explains how the material will be useful in finding a job, building a rewarding career, or succeeding in life.

Set the Pace: Before beginning a chapter it is important to determine what you already know about the topic. *Set the Pace* asks you to think about your own experiences with the subject.

Chapter Objectives: These are your goals for the chapter. When you have done the reading and the work for each chapter, you should have learned about and practiced each of the bulleted skills. These *Objectives* will be revisited in the *Chapter Summary*.

Beginning Each Section

Reading and Study Tip: Each tip presents a helpful suggestion to aid your retention of the material in the section.

In Each Section

Quotations: These thoughts offer inspiration, context, and perspective from important and influential people in all walks of life.

Vocabulary: Important terms are called out in the margins and defined.

New Attitudes/New Opportunities: These profiles present real people giving voice to their real-world goals, concerns, and experiences.

Pace Points: Techniques and advice that I have found useful from my own work experience.

Judgment Call: These real-world scenarios call on you to interpret and act on the information in the section. Check your answers online at www.mhhe.com/pace.

Dr. Joe Pace: These are quotations from my workshops that, over time, my students have found the most meaningful.

Ending Each Section

Quick Recap: Here is a summary to help you review the section material, check yourself with short review questions, and check your answers online at www.mhhe.com/pace.

Chapter Review and Activities

Chapter Summary: The *Chapter Objectives* reappear here with a review of what you should know about each section and about each *Objective*.

Business Vocabulary: All the vocabulary terms from the chapter are listed and defined at the end of the chapter. Double-check to make sure you know what each word means and how it is used.

Key Concept Review: Short answer questions in the *Key Concept Review* will help you remember the material from each section.

Online Project: Go online to learn more about what you have learned in the chapter.

Step Up the Pace case studies: These real-world scenarios help you think about applying what you have learned in the chapter to your own life, job, and career.

Business Skills Brush-Up: This activity gives you the chance to practice important business skills like critical reading and effective writing.

Support for The Professional Development Series

The books of the *Series* are supported by:

Professional Development Series **Website (www.mhhe.com/pace):** On the website, students can find answers to questions posed in the text,

additional chapter review materials, and topics for additional reading and study. Instructors can also access sample syllabi, suggested test questions, and tips for teaching.

Study Smart **Study Skills Tutorial:** From time management to taking notes, *Study Smart* is an excellent way to practice your skills. *Study Smart* was developed by Andrea Bonner and Mieke Schipper of Sir Sanford Fleming College and is available on CD-ROM (0-07-245515-2). This innovative study skills tutorial teaches students essential note-taking methods, test-taking strategies, and time management secrets. Study Smart is free when packaged with the books of *The Professional Development Series.*

Business Week **Online:** Interested instructors can offer their students 15 weeks of access to *Business Week Online* by requesting that a password card be packaged with the books of *The Professional Development Series.* For further information call 1-800-338-3987 or speak to your McGraw-Hill Sales Representative.

Instructor's Resource **CD-ROM:** This is a thorough guide to planning, organizing, and administering courses using *The Professional Development Series.* The CD includes sample syllabi model assessments and test questions, and teaching tips for each section in every chapter of all four books.

About the Author

For over thirty-six years, Dr. Joe Pace has been a nationally recognized speaker, author, and educator. A psychologist and former college president, Dr. Pace currently serves as the Managing Partner of the Education Initiative for The Pacific Institute.

Dr. Pace is creator of the *Success Strategies for Effective Colleges and Schools* program implemented world wide in over 200 colleges and schools. He has served as Commissioner of the Accrediting Council of Independent Colleges and Schools (ACICS) in Washington, D.C.; The Board of Directors of The Association of Independent Colleges and Schools, now known as the CCA (Career College Association); and as President of the Florida Association of Postsecondary Schools and Colleges.

A popular keynote speaker at conferences and conventions, Dr. Pace has also conducted a variety of seminars and workshops throughout North America on such topics as school management, faculty development, student retention, psychology, and motivation. Thousands of college-level students have benefited from his expertise in the areas of psychology, personal development, and business administration.

Dr. Pace is known for his warmth, enthusiasm, humor, and his 'intelligent heart.' His audiences enjoy his genuine spirit and heartwarming stories. Because of his loving and caring nature, Dr. Pace is able to help people to succeed in their chosen careers, but more importantly, to succeed in life.

Acknowledgements

The energy to develop this series has come from my family: my wife Sharon, my daughters Tami and Tiffany, my son-in-law John and my grandkids Nicholas, Jessica, Dylan and Jonathan. Their love and support gets me up in the morning, inspires my work, and excites me about tomorrow.

Thanks also to Shawn Knieriem, my Director of Operations, for her assistance and support with this project.

My special thanks to the Advisory Board and Review Panel for their excellent suggestions, tips, techniques, and wisdom. Also, for their time and effort in attending various meetings. I have considered them friends and colleagues for many years and it was an honor to work with them on this project.

Advisory Board: In October of 2002, a group of educators came together to chart the course for the project that would become *The Professional Development Series.* Their insights and vision guided me.

Teresa Beatty, ECPI

Gary Carlson, ITT Educational Services

Jerry Gallentine, National American University

Gery Hochanadel, Keiser College

Jim Howard, Sanford Brown Colleges

Ken Konesco, Indiana Business Colleges

Review Panel: Once the Board provided the goal, the Review Panel undertook to develop the project. Their sage advice influenced every page of *The Professional Development Series.*

Steve Calabro, Southwest Florida College

JoAnna Downey, Corinthian Colleges

Barb Gillespie, Cuyamaca College

Lynn Judy, Carteret Community College

Ken Konesco, Indiana Business Colleges

Ada Malcioln, International Institute of the Americas

Dena Montiel, Santa Ana School of Continuing Education

Peggy Patlan, Fox College

Sharon Roseman, Computer Career Center

Peggy Schlechter, National American University

The Workplace

1

Get Started

What Will You Do?

1.1 Researching Jobs and Careers Discover that setting goals for your career is the first step to becoming successful; learn how to find the information you need to get started.

1.2 Writing a Résumé Learn to distinguish among the different types of résumés and how to write one that will say everything you want it to say.

1.3 Promoting Yourself Examine small ways to promote yourself that could make a big difference at the office. Learn the importance of a portfolio.

1.4 Networking Learn how to build a network even if you think you don't know anyone.

1.5 Interviewing with Confidence Learn the art of the interview and strategies of negotiation.

Why It's Important

Taking the time to prepare for your job search will pay great dividends. When you have a goal in mind, it's easy to know where to begin. Researching the companies you'll be interviewing with will give you the power to negotiate. Potential employers will be impressed that you took the time to get to know them before you interviewed.

Set the *Pace*

Research Think about a time when you had to research information. Maybe it was for a term paper on a subject with which you were unfamiliar.

• What strategies did you use to do your research?
• Where did you begin?
• Where did you look for sources?

Activity Work in groups of three and share your research strategies. As a group, create the ideal research strategy. Make a chart showing each step and present it to the class.

Researching Jobs and Careers

Landing the ideal job is like following a road map to that one perfect piece of paradise. However, what is paradise for one is not always paradise for another. Sometimes you take a detour away from the intended path in order to follow another. Maybe you run into an obstacle in your path. Can you climb over it? Can you find another way around? You may ask yourself, what do I need to do to get back on the path? Am I willing to take those steps? Or, am I willing to go in another direction? These are questions successful career builders must ask themselves along the way.

Go For It! A **goal** is something you put effort into achieving. Goals are always easier to reach when you know the way. You will encounter obstacles, but you are better prepared to meet and overcome those obstacles when you have a goal in sight.

goal something you put effort into achieving

♦♦ *Don't compromise yourself. You are all you've got.* ♫♫

Janis Joplin
American Rock and Folk Singer

Being Knowledgeable and Practical

Most successful people know their own strengths and weaknesses. They use those strengths to reach their goals. Their weaknesses may never need to come into play. Some choose to turn a weakness into a strength in order to obtain a goal they never thought possible.

Know Yourself

Your first step should be to write a list of your strengths and weaknesses, your interests, your education, your experiences, and your career and personal goals for 5 and 10 years from now. Then, think about the type of work environment in which you would feel most comfortable.

- Do you like the challenge of meeting deadlines?
- Are you willing to work frequent overtime hours?
- Are you willing to travel?
- How much traveling are you willing to do?
- Do you enjoy frequent contact with people?
- Do you enjoy working on a team?
- Do you prefer to work alone?

Getting to know yourself helps make your goals real. When you define who you are, what you can and cannot do, and what you want to do, you light the way to a well-planned and successful future.

Getting Practical

After you have gotten to know yourself—your strengths and weaknesses, your goals, your education, your experiences, and so forth—you are ready to get practical about your ideal job. Every "ideal" job has practical characteristics that you need to consider.

For example, if you are a single parent rearing two children alone, you may dream about a career that includes international travel. But for practical reasons, you may not want to spend that much time away from home and your children. Instead of traveling yourself, you decide that you could help other people with their travel plans by becoming a travel agent. Besides helping others with their travel plans, your need for travel could be satisfied by well-planned vacations.

The ideal and the practical meet when you compare all the things you know about yourself. You need to ask yourself:

- What type of position do I want?
- What size company do I want to work for?
- What benefits am I looking for? Think about insurance, vacation, flexible schedules, on-site daycare, sick leave, retirement savings plans, and pensions.
- What is my desired salary range?
- In what size community am I prepared to live?
- How much travel, if any, am I willing to do?
- Do I want additional training or education to better my chances for promotion?
- Am I willing to transfer if asked to do so?

It's important to be realistic about salary goals. The community in which you work will affect the size of your salary. Often, salaries are based on local cost-of-living statistics. **Cost-of-living statistics** are based on the price people in an area pay for products and services, such as housing, food, utilities, and transportation. A company in a small community rarely offers big-city salaries. A small company may not offer as many opportunities for promotions, transfers, or travel. But a small company may be more willing to offer flexible schedules or more sick leave for working parents.

cost-of-living statistics statistics based on the price people in an area pay for products and services such as housing, food, utilities, and transportation

Your Search

Now that you have your goals in hand and know the type of company you want to work for, you need to find that company. Fortunately, there are many time-saving resources out there.

To begin a successful search, decide which companies to target. The best way to do this is to begin by researching what's out there. The Internet offers many tools for job seekers. A few years ago, Internet job sites offered information about a limited number of careers, mainly highly specialized and technical jobs with large companies. Today, you can find many more types of job listings—military jobs, entry-level positions, internships, and volunteer opportunities—with many small and medium-sized companies.

« Each of us has a fire in our hearts for something. It's our goal in life to find it and to keep it lit. »

Mary Lou Retton
American Olympic Gold Medal–Winning Gymnast

Focus and Organize

After you have looked at what's out there, the next step is to brainstorm as many possibilities as you can. Target about five companies to research further.

Organization is the key to a successful job search. Keep records of your job search near the telephone (see Figure 1.1). When you begin to receive calls from your targets, you'll be better able to give intelligent answers and make a good impression. Along with your records, keep printouts of the advertisements to which you responded. You also should keep your résumés, your research findings on the company, your follow-up letters, and anything asked for in the advertisement, that is, the cover letter, salary requirements, references, letters of recommendation, writing samples, and so forth.

Figure 1.1 *Job Search Record*

Company	Contact	Phone No./Fax E-mail	Position Applied for	Résumé Sent	Date Sent	Follow-up Sent
Company A	Mr. Grimes	212-555-0522 (Tele) 212-555-0521 (Fax) grimes@companya.com	Paralegal	Version 1	10/28/07	3/13/08
Company B	Ms. Fields	212-555-0623	Research Assistant	Version 2	10/15/07	3/29/08
Company C	Mrs. Ono	212-555-9685 onohr@companyc.com	Research	Version 2	10/15/07	3/29/08
Company D	Ms. Ruffing	212-555-1678 (Tele) 212-555-0622 (Fax) ruffingk@companyd.com	Paralegal Assistant	Version 1	11/01/07	4/15/08
Company E	Mr. Stackhouse	212-555-7848	Legal Administrative Assistant	Version 3	11/04/07	4/18/08

Thinking Critically When you begin to receive calls from your targets, having the information in front of you helps you make a good first impression. *What other information might you add to a job search record?*

JUDGEMENT CALL

Persistence

Your Challenge

You are looking for a new job. You have several options and don't really know how to go about it. You would like to find a job that you really like with a company you respect but don't know where to start. You have a little money and a lot of time, so you are in a position to do a good search. What do you do?

The Possibilities

A) File for unemployment, then stay home and watch soaps all day long.

B) Mail your résumé to all the companies in the classified ads and HR departments of companies you have heard of, then sit back and wait for a response.

C) Call people you know, look for want ads in store windows, and take the first job you can find. Worry about your career later.

D) Do research, find four or five companies you like, use your network to find a contact at each, and work on getting informational interviews with each one. Send out your résumé and follow up with a call and/or an e-mail until you get a response.

Your Solution

Choose the solution that you think will be most effective and write a few sentences explaining your opinion. Then check your answer with the answer on our Web site: **www.mhhe.com/pace.**

Go Online

The Internet is quickly becoming the most time-saving and cost-effective way for employees to look for work—and for employers to look for workers. Companies with Web sites often have employment sites where you can post a résumé or see what positions are available within the company. If you don't have access to the Internet, you can find help at many public libraries.

Many Internet employment sites offer other services—some are free and others charge a small fee. Other sites offer space for you to post your résumé so that employers may see it. Services may include such career tools as

- Résumé writing help.
- Online educational help.
- Newsletters.
- Career advice.
- Company profiles.

Network

A personal search requires the use of a network. A **network** consists of people you know and with whom you can share valuable information. Many experts agree that "networking" is one of the most successful ways to find work. Let people within your network know what kind of work you want. Also let them know when you'll be available.

Periodic contact is the key to maintaining an active network. Many salespeople keep a contact's personal information, such as birthdays, names and ages of children, spouse's name, and so forth, on note cards. A network contact who feels valued will be more willing to share information.

network people you know and with whom you can share valued information

Personal Network The people who make up your personal network are your family, friends, neighbors, casual acquaintances, and teachers or counselors—anyone you know on a personal level. Family members and friends who work for a company you are interested in are likely to know about any positions that may be open. They also will know the correct person for you to contact. Teachers and counselors are often contacted by local businesses and asked to recommend people to fill vacant positions.

Professional Network Your professional network is made up of people you have worked with, whether through part-time employment, summer jobs, or internships. A professional network contact can be used as a reference of past work experience. A professional network also includes people you know from civic and professional organizations to which you belong. They are people you meet at a conference or seminar and with whom you strike up a conversation and exchange contact information.

Career Placement

Most colleges and universities offer career placement services for their students. This office lists employment ads for part- and full-time positions available with local businesses. They host job fairs to bring students in contact with companies. Other services provided by career placement centers usually include résumé creation and help with interviewing skills. Many provide job-related computer programs, books, pamphlets, and magazines.

Private Agencies

Most cities have private agencies that are used by local employers to fill a variety of positions. Some agencies focus on one area, such as filling office positions. The company looking for employees pays a fee to the agency, which is usually a percentage of the annual salary for the position.

Other private agencies, known as temporary (temp) agencies, seek employees who are willing to work for a short period of time. Some temp employees help companies who have a need for short-time workers, usually in order to fulfill a customer order. If the company's need becomes extended, full-time workers may be chosen from the temp staff. Other companies use temp agencies as a way to find good employees to hire. Temp agencies are a good way to get your foot in the door. They are also a good way to try out a position before committing to it as a career.

Newspapers

Newspaper classifieds are the traditional place one looks when searching for work. The Sunday paper usually has the most job listings. You may buy a subscription to a local newspaper or simply visit your local library, which usually subscribes to several area newspapers. Many large-city newspapers have online sites that publish their current classifieds. These sites have search capabilities, so you don't need to spend a lot of time online looking through every ad in order to find a specific position.

Professional Journals and Books

The best place to look for specialized career information is in specialized journals, which can be found at your local library and in bookstores. For example, *Publisher's Weekly* lists advertisements for writers, editors, and graphic artists.

Your local library is an excellent, low-cost source for career research. Job or business directories list information such as company name, address, and telephone number; number of employees; the names of the senior officers; total sales volume; and so on. These books are usually found in the reference section. Reference books cannot be borrowed, so be sure to bring along money for photocopies.

Analyzing Companies and Benefits

You have done your research. You have found five companies to target. Your next step is to look at your target companies to see if they fit your goals and expectations. Are there some goals and expectations you can modify in order to work for this company? Will you need further training? Will you need to relocate?

Many company Web sites publish their benefit programs online. Benefits are a large part of the reward or payment system. Make sure the benefits are what you need. Do you like the company even though it does not offer dental insurance? Can you live with that? Use your list of goals and expectations to see if each company's benefits are a fit for you.

Learning Company Structure and Locating Your Place

Networking is a great tool for learning a company's structure. People who work for a company in which you are interested can tell you about the company structure.

Most companies have a structure that looks like a pyramid. At the top is the chief executive officer or CEO, or a chief financial officer or CFO. All other managers and employees fall into place below them. See Figure 1.2 for a sample company structure.

Figure 1.2 *Company Structure*

Joan Hansen CEO		
Thom Keaner VP, Sales		**Julie Sponaugle** VP, Operations
Vonda Johnson District Sales Manager		**Keith Alt** Customer Service Manager
Ray Seven Plant Manager	**Phillip MacKay** Warehouse Manager	**Sandy McGovern** Human Resource Manager
Anna Goldberg Accounting Manager	**Kevin Marinalli** Accounting Assistant	**Laray Masters** Accounting Assistant
Maria Alvarez Customer Service Representative	**Tammy Johnson** Customer Service Representative	**Jonah Weinstein** Customer Service Representative
Lashonda Underwood Sales Representative	**Donnie Freedman** Sales Representative	**Sharon Anderson** Sales Representative
Kathy Wu Shift Manager	**Craig Stine** Inventory Manager	**Mathew James** Maintenance
Dave Keith Human Resource Assistant		**Ryan Cooper** Human Resource Assistant
Toby Au Line Manager		

Thinking Critically You know your place when you know company structure. *How else might a company structure look?*

RESEARCHING JOBS AND CAREERS

Now you should have a better idea of the benefits and importance of researching. Here is a quick summary of why such preparation is important.

• Having a plan helps you reach your goals.

• Knowing how to use resources wisely saves time.

• Networking is an important tool in a successful job search.

• Researching a company you are interested in makes you knowledgeable.

CHECK YOURSELF

1. Name three resources you can use to do a local search.

2. Describe the importance of creating and maintaining a personal and professional network.

Check your answers online at **www.mhhe.com/pace.**

BUSINESS VOCABULARY

cost-of-living statistics   statistics based on the price people in an area pay for products and services such as housing, food, utilities, and transportation

goal   something you put effort into achieving

network   people you know and with whom you can share valued information

Writing a Résumé

Writing your résumé is one of the single most important parts of your job search. It may be the first opportunity you have to grab the attention of an employer. It's usually the first and only chance you have to make a good impression.

What Is A Résumé? Your résumé is a reflection of you. It is a history of your career that lists your jobs and activities. It also shows how well you are able to communicate your skills and experience. It's a chance to sell yourself and your skills. It's a chance for you to tell the employer why you deserve the job more than the hundreds of other people who also sent résumés.

Attention to Detail

Did you use proper grammar, spelling, and punctuation? Nothing sends your résumé to the trashcan faster than errors and careless mistakes. Careful preparation of a résumé is a key to your employment success. Learn how to create a résumé that targets a potential employer.

Résumé Structure

The general structure of all résumés is basically the same: name and contact information, career objective, education, special skills, and work experience. You can still create many different styles and formats using this structure. Make your document as clear and easy to read as possible. If potential employers cannot find important information about you quickly and easily, they will probably throw away your résumé!

- **The name and contact information** contains your name, address, telephone number, fax number, and e-mail address. If your address is temporary, be sure to indicate when you will be moving and how a potential employer can contact you after your move date. Do not add a personal Web site unless it looks professional and has to do with your career.
- **The objective,** which is optional, states the goal of your résumé. If you are sending résumés to several companies, keep your objective general, such as *Objective: A career in information technology.* If you are targeting a specific position, make your objective fit the position. For example, if you are applying for a position as fundraising development coordinator with a nonprofit organization, this should be your objective: ***Objective: Position with a nonprofit organization, helping to develop successful fundraising campaigns and managing diverse volunteer activities.***
- **Your education** should begin with your most recent experience first, especially if you have attended several colleges. If you are currently

> ### Reading and Study Tip
>
> ***Headings***
> Read the headings in this section. How are they similar to the headings in a résumé? Write a sentence or two explaining how they are used and why they are useful.

attending college, list that one first. Include college, degree, major, grade point average or GPA (only if it is 3.2 or higher), and your expected date of graduation.

- **Special skills,** which is optional, is a chance for you to list specific skills, such as computer programs you know how to use, foreign languages you speak, and any special training you may have.

- List your most current **work experience** first and then work your way backward. Include the months and years of employment, company name, and the position you held and describe the work you did for the company. When describing your experiences, you should be brief and specific. Use action verbs, such as those listed below, to highlight each experience to its best advantage.

Action Verbs That Show Leadership Skills	Action Verbs That Show Communication Skills	Action Verbs That Show Organizational Skills
directed	answered	arranged
enlisted	appraised	assembled
formed	briefed	catalogued
founded	conducted	coordinated
hired	contacted	distributed
initiated	demonstrated	executed
instituted	drafted	formalized
led	educated	implemented
managed	explained	installed
moderated	informed	maintained
motivated	instructed	organized
presided over	interviewed	planned
represented	lectured	prepared
staged	listened	processed
started	presented	recorded
supervised	reported	reorganized
	taught	routed
	translated	scheduled
	wrote	updated

Internet Quest

Sample Résumés

Visit online job sites that display sample résumés. See how many résumés use action words and analyze how they are used. Find four phrases to describe yourself and your skills and use them in your résumé.

References

References should not be listed on your résumé. It is assumed that you can and will supply them if requested. Create a separate sheet of paper listing your references' names, addresses, job titles, e-mail addresses, and telephone numbers. Choose references carefully—people who can talk about you personally and about your work record but who are not related to you. Ask for permission first before using someone as a reference. Remember, they are part of your network. Always let them know when you have accepted a position and thank them for their help.

New Attitudes / New Opportunities

Meet Georgia Donati. Georgia is the retired supervising librarian of the Mid-Manhattan Library Job Information Center in New York City. The Center contains a growing collection of career-related materials. These materials deal with such subjects as choosing a career, conducting a job search, writing résumés, and researching employers. Georgia now works there as a career resources counselor. She uses the library's resources to help job seekers. Here's what she has to say about . . .

What a résumé tells a potential employer. "A résumé is a snapshot of yourself at one point in your life. It gives a brief history of who you are and what you have done. Include a cover letter as a complement to your résumé. The résumé is like a skeleton that has clothing on it, but the cover letter contains the embellishments—like your jewelry. The cover letter explains in more detail what you are all about.

Your goal in writing a résumé is to sell an employer. Its purpose is to get you to the interview stage. A résumé won't work unless you know where to send it. Where you send the résumé is almost as important as what you write in it. Research the person you send your résumé to, so if you do get an interview, you will know what to say and what to ask. Show that you are interested enough to have done research about the company."

The first thing she looks for in a good résumé. "The most important element is a simple, one-sentence summary of the person's qualifications—the bucket of skills and personal traits he or she has to offer. This should be at the top of the résumé; this will catch the eye of the person reviewing it. State your objective at the top, too. The objective tells what you want. It's like an arrow flying towards the bull's eye and the rest of the résumé should enhance that objective."

The most common mistakes people make on their résumés. "Many résumés are too impersonal. I find that many job seekers list everything they have ever done in a "laundry list." Your résumé should be much more targeted in terms of your objective. Also, a résumé can be too cluttered. Visually it has to be attractive with enough white space and bulleted lists. Long paragraphs will leave the HR person glassy-eyed. Be selective in what you present. Only include what you can contribute to the job and show that you can do things that add value to an organization."

If it is ever okay to exaggerate. "Never exaggerate because people do check. They'll find out if you aren't honest. When people have gaps in their work history, I say, be honest about it. These days, it's not a terrible thing to have a gap in your work history. For example, if someone has been out of the workforce to have children, she should include that in her résumé. People with experience they didn't get paid for often feel as if they have nothing to offer. I always tell people to put their volunteer or real-life experiences in the résumé listed by skill. Planning, teaching, managing, and scheduling are all skills that people who run a household have that are also useful in the workplace."

Paper Résumés

Paper résumés are the traditional form of résumé. They can be sent in the mail or faxed to a prospective employer. A paper résumé lets you choose the type of paper and the formatting that best gets your message across. There are three types of paper résumés: chronological, functional, and combination.

Chronological résumés

chronological résumé lists education and experiences with the most
recent listed first

The **chronological résumé** lists education and experiences beginning with the most recent. This type of résumé is useful when you have had steady employment and experience in your area of interest (see Figure 1.3).

Pace Points

Résumé Follow Through
Don't just mail your résumé and forget about it. Follow up. Call a week after you sent it to check that it was received. The person on the phone will pull it out to have a look and then put it back at the top of the pile. This way you are sure that it gets seen and the person associates your résumé with the friendly and polite person on the phone.

Figure 1.3 *Chronological Résumé*

Tilda Smith
2738 East Fifth Street
Tiffin, Ohio 44883
E-mail: ttssmith@two.net

EXPERIENCE   **Evening Desk Manager**
Days Inn, Tiffin, Ohio
September 2000 to present

- Check in guests
- Field guest service calls
- Schedule guest reservations for conventions and special events

Day Shift Manager
JoJo's Burgers, Tiffin, Ohio
June 1998 to September 2000

- Hired shift personnel
- Managed and supervised 10 full-time employees
- Scheduled shift workers and maintenance crew

EDUCATION   Associate of Arts Degree to be awarded May 10, 2003
North Central State College, Mansfield, Ohio
Major: Hospitality Management
GPA: 3.75

SPECIAL SKILLS Proficient with Microsoft Word, PowerPoint, and Excel
Received specialized customer service training at current position

Thinking Critically This résumé lists skills with the most recent first. *Could Tilda have presented her information differently?*

Functional

A **functional résumé** is used when you want to emphasize education and training over experience. Your previous experience may be in a career that is very different from the path you have now chosen. You want to focus on the skills and education you are now receiving (see Figure 1.4).

functional résumé emphasizes education and training over experience

---

Figure 1.4 *Functional Résumé*

Lin Chen
27 Calumet Ave.
Valparaiso, Indiana 46383
219-555-7606
E-mail: lcdragon@chi.net

Objective: Position in the field of data management systems

Coursework:
• Integrated Management Strategies
• Data Sources
• Statistics I-IV

Special Skills:
• Bilingual: Fluent in Vietnamese and English
• Proficient with Microsoft Word, PowerPoint, and Excel
• Received customer service training at Valparaiso High School Adult Education

Experience: Server
Kelsey's, Valparaiso, Indiana
June 2000 to Present
• Took meal orders
• Worked with kitchen to assure customer satisfaction
• Assured that station was clean and orderly

Cashier
Wiseway Supermarket, Valparaiso, Indiana
June 1998 to June 2000

Interests: Snorkeling
Travel

References: Available upon request

Thinking Critically A functional résumé highlights skills and training. *What else could Lin have added to her résumé?*

Combination

combination résumé emphasizes skills and education as well as work experience

The **combination résumé** uses the best of both the chronological and functional. It emphasizes skills and education as well as work experience (see Figure 1.5).

Figure 1.5 *Combination Résumé*

Carlos Montana
175 West Aspen
Flagstaff, Arizona 86004
928-555-7606
E-mail: cmwh@az.net

Objective: Position in the field of Hospitality Management with a world-class resort or hotel

Special Skills: Proficient in Spanish and English
Proficient with Microsoft Word, PowerPoint, and Excel

Experience: *Evening Desk Manager*
Comfort Inn, Flagstaff, Arizona
September 2000 to present

• Check in guests
• Field guest service calls
• Schedule guest reservations for conventions and special events

Day Shift Manager
Black Bart's Steakhouse, Flagstaff, Arizona
June 1998 to September 2000

• Hired shift personnel
• Managed and supervised 10 full-time employees
• Scheduled shift workers and maintenance crew

Education: Associate of Arts Degree to be awarded May 10, 2003
Coconino Community College, Flagstaff, Arizona
Major: Hospitality Management
GPA: 3.80

Honors and Dean's List, four quarters
Activities: Therapeutic riding volunteer
Red Cross Volunteer

Thinking Critically This résumé emphasizes skills and education as well as work experience. *When would you be most likely to use this type of résumé?*

The Electronic Résumé

The **electronic résumé** contains no italics, underlining, bullets, or any type of formatting (Figure 1.6). Use the electronic résumé when you need to e-mail a résumé to a potential employer or when you post to online databases and employment sites.

electronic résumé used when posting online or sending via e-mail; contains no formatting

Figure 1.6 *Electronic Résumé*

```
JUAN HERNANDEZ
15 Main Street
Apt. 2B
Los Angeles, California 77254
(213) 555-1852
(213) 555-1724 Fax
juanh@webmail.com

JOB OBJECTIVE:
A senior management position in the data analysis field

SPECIAL SKILLS:
Proficient with PC-based programs, databases, and systems using Excel,
PowerPoint, Access, and Visual BASIC.
Proficient in both Spanish and English. Additional training in
statistics, management/leadership strategies, and Web site design.

PROFESSIONAL EXPERIENCE:
1997 to Present
MicroKey Data Systems, Los Angeles, CA
Data Systems Analyst II
Helped develop new processes for more efficient data retrieval system.
Developed system to cut department costs by 35 percent on all new projects.
Acted as Spanish language translator with international clients.
Created company Web site portion for Spanish users.

1994 to 1997
Texsystems, Dallas, TX
Junior Data Analyst
Developed system to cut department costs by 25 percent.
Developed a system to cut inventory insurance costs by 16 percent.

EDUCATION:
San Francisco State University, San Francisco, CA
Master of Science in Business Administration with emphasis in
Business Analysis/Operations Research
```

Thinking Critically This résumé is used when posting online or sending via e-mail. It contains no formatting. *What form does this résumé take?*

❝ *Put it before them* briefly *so they will read it,* clearly *so they will appreciate it,* picturesquely *so they will remember it and, above all,* accurately *so they will be guided by its light.* ❞

Joseph Pulitzer
Hungarian/American Journalist and Newspaper Publisher; Namesake of the Pulitzer Prize for Literature and Journalism

Basic Requirements and Helpful Tips

The purpose of your résumé is to catch the eye of the employer. It is usually the first contact you have with the employer. Proper formatting and arrangement of information on the page can help the busy employer target your message quickly and clearly.

- Try not to make your résumé longer than one page. Be brief with your experience descriptions. You can expand on your experience in the interview. If you need another page to keep your résumé from being crowded, put your name on the top right-hand corner of the second page.
- Do not staple extra résumé pages, the cover letter, or other items to the résumé.
- Use a 1.5-inch top margin and 1-inch side and bottom margins.
- Use good-quality paper with matching envelopes for your résumé and cover letter. Use a light, neutral color such as cream or gray.
- Use bold and capital letters for your headings.

Tips From a Mentor

Ten Résumé No No's

- *Don't exaggerate your skills or experience on your résumé. Lying about yourself or your skills or experience is grounds for dismissal.*

- *Don't include personal information such as age, height, weight, sex, marital or family status, race, and religious/political preference.*

- *Don't include references on your résumé. Type them on a separate sheet of paper so that you can present them if your potential employer asks for them.*

- *Don't use the first person and possessive pronouns: I, me, my, mine, or our.*

- *Don't send errors and typos. Do not rely on your computer's spell-check and grammar check.*

- *Don't send it without double-checking your contact information, dates of employment, and so forth. It's difficult for someone to contact you if you leave off your telephone number or write it incorrectly.*

- *Don't rely on templates and wizards. They look fake, lack flexibility for each individual's needs, have out-of-date formats, and make editing and layout changes difficult and frustrating.*

- *Don't concentrate entirely on job duties. Accomplishments and achievements show an employer how you can contribute to a company's bottom line.*

- *Don't send a résumé for a position for which you are not qualified. If a job ad lists requirements you do not have, don't waste your time—or theirs.*

- *Don't get carried away being creative. Avoid frilly fonts, stickers, stamps, colored pens, handwriting, lots of white out, or too-small type. Your résumé should be clean, clearly organized, readable, and professional.*

- Use an easily read font such as Helvetica, Palatino, or Times in 11- or 12-point size for the text and 14-point size for the headings.
- Send original printed résumés; never send photocopies.
- After you finish your résumé and have checked it for spelling, grammar, and spacing issues, have another person look it over. Because you have been working closely with it, you may not see errors that will be obvious to others.

Tailoring Your Résumé

The wise job hunter has not one, but several versions of his or her résumé. No one single résumé fits every position. All companies have different needs and different structures. You will need to stress different skills for different positions. For example, requirements for a proofreader in the printing industry will differ from the requirements for a proofreader in the publishing industry. The proofreader in the printing industry will need to know how to read printing plates, how to check for plate/color registration, and how a book is physically constructed. The publishing proofreader will need to check for grammar, spelling, punctuation rules, house style, and consistency.

It's best to have a generic résumé, or one that contains your general information. When you need a specialized résumé, rearrange the generic one to highlight the skills and experience you have that fit the position. Keep a copy of all the résumés you send out.

Take the time to sit down and review your personal history. Recording your personal history will help transform your generic résumé into the résumé that fits the position. Remember to keep all your job search information together by using a job search record (see Figure 1.1).

Personal History List

Having this information at hand can make it easier for you to tailor your résumé to fit yours and the employer's needs. Make certain your résumé is focused on the employer, industry, or position for which you apply.

- List your education: high school and college.
  - Name and location.
  - Dates of attendance.
  - Degree or diploma.
  - Major(s) or course of study.
  - Minor.
  - Overall GPA.
  - Major GPA.
  - Class rank.
  - Courses completed and grades received.
  - Academic honors, that is, Dean's list, valedictorian, and so on.
  - Merit-based scholarships.
  - Any other school-based honors and awards.
- List your standardized test scores, such as ACTs and SATs.
- List your work experience for each job you held.
  - Name and address of employer.
  - Type of business.
  - Job title.
  - Dates of employment.

- Reason for leaving.
- Name and telephone number of direct supervisor.
- Major accomplishments.
- New skills and knowledge gained or improved upon.
- List your activities.
  - Name of club, organization, or hobby.
  - Position or title.
  - Dates of involvement.
  - Activities of the organization or club.
  - Major responsibilities and accomplishments.
  - New skills and knowledge gained or improved upon.
- List your skills.
  - Computer knowledge: software, hardware, and programming.
  - Foreign languages: specify degree of proficiency.
  - Math and science: fields of study, lab experience, and so forth.
  - Business: cost accounting, economic forecasting, and so on.
  - Arts: sewing, camera operation, graphic design, and others.

QUICK RECAP 1.2

WRITING A RÉSUMÉ

Now you should have a better idea of the benefits of creating a proper résumé. Here is a quick summary of why this is important.

- When you know the types of résumés, you are better able to create the one that will fit the position you want.
- When you know basic résumé requirements, you can create a résumé that gets your message across quickly and clearly.
- Tailoring your résumé to the position you want lets the employer know that you took extra care and time to look at the company.
- When you take the time to chart your personal history, you don't have to worry about leaving out important details that may better your chances.

CHECK YOURSELF

1. List the three types of paper résumés and how each is structured.
2. Name three helpful tips that will make your résumé easy to read.

Check your answers online at **www.mhhe.com/pace**.

BUSINESS VOCABULARY

chronological résumé   lists education and experiences with the most recent listed first
combination résumé   emphasizes skills and education as well as work experience
electronic résumé   used when posting online or sending via e-mail; contains no formatting
functional résumé   emphasizes education and training over experience

Promoting Yourself

One way of showing your professionalism is to be meticulous in what you wear, how you groom yourself, and how you conduct yourself. When you present yourself well during an interview, you show that you care about your career—that you think you can contribute to the company, that you can solve problems, that you are valuable, that you are the best person for the job.

Sell Yourself.   Whether you are job hunting, asking for a promotion, or taking part in a performance review, you need to market yourself and your skills. Even if you do excellent work, people won't know it unless you tell them. You may have been taught to be humble. However, your employer—or prospective employer—needs to know what you can do for the company. Be your own "salesperson" and sell yourself!

Promoting Yourself as a Professional

Putting your best foot forward as a professional means that you dress and groom properly, use correct manners, communicate clearly, and use proper posture. If you look and act professional, a prospective employer will be more likely to think of you as a professional.

Proper Dress and Grooming

Dressing properly involves choosing clothes, accessories, and shoes that look professional. Choose conservative clothes that are clean, pressed, and spot free. They should not be revealing or too tight. Choose colors that are conservative, such as brown, gray, dark green, or blue. Go easy on the accessories—one ring per hand and one earring per ear. Women should not wear jewelry that dangles or is too flashy. Men should not wear earrings in a professional setting. Piercings and tattoos should be well covered. Make sure your shoes are clean, polished, and comfortable.

 Proper grooming means that your clothes are properly fastened. Your body and breath is clean and odor free. Go easy on the cologne and aftershave. Gum chewing is not a proper habit for professionals.

Correct Manners

The manners you show to the world also reflect on the company for which you work. *Please* and *thank you* are simple ways to express manners. Other matters of manners will depend on your position with the company and your place of employment. A sales associate meets regularly with customers and needs to know the proper handshake, the proper introduction, the proper telephone manners, and the proper table manners.

> **Reading and Study Tip**
>
> *Visual Aids*
> Visuals and graphics can help to illustrate an idea, just like the figures throughout this book and the images in your career portfolio. Find one place in this section where you could use a picture or diagram to explain the text. On a separate sheet of paper, sketch or describe your visual aid.

 ❝ *Defining myself, as opposed to being defined by others, is one of the most difficult challenges I face.* **❞**

 Carol Mosely-Braun
First African-American Woman Elected to the U.S. Senate

A person who does not meet with the public will need to know office manners: arriving on time and prepared for meetings; quickly responding to memos, e-mails, and so forth; meeting with office visitors; respecting desk privacy; limiting office noise; and avoiding negative and offensive office humor. Your office setting will determine the manners you need to get along with others. Keep your eyes and ears open to the messages successful employees give out at your workplace.

Clear Communication

Clear and proper communication is key to putting your best professional foot forward. When talking, avoid using slang and improper grammar. Avoid sexist, discriminatory, or labeling words and phrases, such as "honey" or "girls" or "best man for the job." Use "women" or "best person for the job." Choose the proper words and facial expressions to express what you want to say. Be concise; no one wants to listen to a long-winded explanation when two or three well-worded sentences will do.

Approach your writing in the same manner as you do your speech. Make sure your written communications contain all information needed by all parties who will read it. Well-written memos, reports, and e-mails say what needs to be said the first time. Remember that anything in writing may come back to haunt you—choose your words and message carefully.

Posture

Posture can say many things about a person. It can demonstrate confidence or lack of it. A person who walks, stands, and sits with a straight back, shoulders back, head held erect, and eyes forward shows confidence. A person who walks,

Figure 1.7 *You Be the Judge*

Juanita's Approach	Sandra's Approach
Returns to her desk after breaks and lunch	Takes long breaks and lunches
Desk is neat and organized	Desk is sloppy and unorganized
Dresses professionally	Dresses unprofessionally
Calls to make an appointment	Stops by unannounced
Communicates well	Communicates poorly
Gives careful thought to her résumé	Throws together her résumé
Arrives on time for meeting	Arrives late for meeting

Thinking Critically Which woman is most likely to get the assistant manager position? *What advice would you give to Sandra?*

stands, and sits with rounded back, slumped shoulders, and nose and eyes toward the ground shows a lack of confidence. As a professional, you should show confidence.

Posture also tells people if you are listening. A person who sits up straight in his or her chair with both feet on the ground and both hands on the table shows that he or she is open to listening. A person slumped in his or her chair with legs bouncing nervously and crossed arms is not listening.

Your Career in a Portfolio of Work

Portfolios are not just for teachers, artists, models, and actors anymore. Today, professionals in just about every field can create and put to good use a portfolio of their work. Your portfolio is useful for "showing" your skills during an interview. A **portfolio** is an organized sampling of the work you have done in your career. It shows off your good work habits, your creativity, your technical skills, and your contribution to the company.

portfolio an organized sampling of the work you have done in your career

How Your Portfolio Can Get You a Job

The smart professional jobseeker creates and maintains a portfolio to present at interviews. A portfolio can "show" what cannot be said in your résumé. A public relations professional would include examples of his or her strongest press releases. A marketing professional would include examples of his or her most successful media and advertising campaigns.

How Your Portfolio Can Get You Promoted

When used at a performance review, a portfolio can "show" why you deserve a raise or promotion. It can remind the manager that you made changes to the company Web site that made it easier for customers to place orders, which increased orders and profits. Your portfolio can remind the hospital administrator that you increased the number of volunteers working in the Candy Stripe program. It is physical proof of why you deserve a raise.

Putting Together a Sample of Your Work

Use only high-quality items in your portfolio, no photocopies. Use a nice binder and place your documents in plastic sheet protectors. Do not laminate your documents. Your portfolio can be structured in a way that best represents you, but most portfolios contain the following items:

- Introduction or title page
- Table of contents
- Divider pages with tabs
- Résumé
- References
- Diplomas
- Certificates
- Awards
- Transcript of grades (if 3.2 or higher)
- Letters of recommendation
- Examples of your creativity and efforts, such as bulletin boards, lesson plans, company/school newsletters, marketing campaigns, production procedures, Web page design, budget planning, community service, and so forth.

Experts recommend that you have no more than 10 samples. Any more could be too much for the person looking at your portfolio. Include only your best letters of recommendation.

Presenting Your Portfolio

Present your portfolio near the end of your interview. Tell the interviewer at the beginning that you have brought your portfolio and would like to talk about it later. Because your time may be limited, prepare two well-worded comments for each page. Take time to rehearse your portfolio presentation. This will show the interviewer that you came prepared.

QUICK RECAP 1.3

PROMOTING YOURSELF

Now you should have a better idea of the benefits and importance of creating a professional image. Here is a quick summary.
- A professional dresses and grooms properly, uses correct manners, communicates clearly, and uses good posture.
- A portfolio "shows" what you have accomplished in your career.
- Preparing a brief presentation of your portfolio demonstrates your preparedness.

CHECK YOURSELF

1. Why is it important for the professional to practice proper dress and grooming habits?
2. When would you use a portfolio?

Check your answers online at **www.mhhe.com/pace.**

BUSINESS VOCABULARY

portfolio   an organized sampling of the work you have done in your career

Networking

When the job market is tight or you are new to a career field, networking can be your best bet for job hunting. A good network provides you with vital information on job openings, new positions, new trends, and so on. A good network can give you the edge because you'll have lots of people putting in a good word for you. Build your network, love it, feed it, and you'll be rewarded.

It's Not **What** *You Know.*   Getting any kind of favor or attention in life often depends on who you know. Make this work to your advantage. You will come to realize in this section just how many people you really do know. Being part of a social network means helping others and allowing them to help you.

How to Develop and Use a Network

In Section 1.1, you learned that a network is made up of people you know and with whom you can share valued information. You may not think you know enough people to have a network. But everyone knows someone through

Reading and Study Tip

Questions
Study the wording of the questions in this section. Will you get only a *yes* or *no* answer? Rewrite *yes* or *no* questions so you get a more detailed response.

- Family and extended family.
- Friends and acquaintances.
- Neighbors.
- Co-workers.
- Past employers.
- High school teachers and college professors.
- High school counselors and college advisors.
- Religious organizations.
- Clubs and community organizations.
- Sports team and health club members.
- Hobbies.

Take the time to make a list of *all* the people you know. This is your network. The people on your list also know other people and have a network of their own.

Develop Your Network

Networks are based on friendly give and take. But all the people in your network don't have to be your friends. The people in your network usually have something to offer you, and you have something to offer them.

People in sales understand the need for a network. Salespeople do favors for others who may help them in the future. They give information back to help keep the bonds of their network strong. Such information can lead to sales and opportunity for both parties. Many salespeople have the gift for putting a face to a name, remembering the names of spouses and children, birthdays, interests, and significant achievements in a person's life. Salespeople also know that it is important to keep their network active. They know how important it is to stay in touch with the people in their network. If you do not have a good memory, one way to remember information about your contacts is to create a networking journal (see Figure 1.8).

Figure 1.8 *Networking Journal*

Name/ Birthday	Phone Number/ E-mail	Company Name	Spouse/ Birthday	Children/ Birthdays	Achievements/ Interests
Jerry Kilgore 8/25/45	120-555-4578 jk@fourstar.com	Four Star Paper, Inc.	Anna 2/8/50	Josh 4/14/84	Ran a marathon 2001
Denise Spielmann 5/6/60	451-555-1245 com1@indy.com	Indy, Inc.	Tom 5/7/57	Elaine Connor 5/1/82 11/8/84	Mountain climber, training for Mt. Everest in 2004
La Shawn Johnson 6/28/74	223-555-6785 ljohnson@kenner.com	Kenner Envelope Co.	Dana 1/2/74	Keith/Kenneth 12/23/92	Collector of African-American art, loves basketball

Thinking Critically A networking journal is the place to record all the details you need to know in order to show the people in your network that you care about them. *What other information could be added to the journal?*

JUDGEMENT CALL

Networking

Your Challenge
You are at a barbeque at your friend's house and you meet his new girlfriend. You find out she works in event planning, which is a job you have always been interested in. You are not looking for a new job at the moment, but you can't see yourself working for your current company forever. You have no experience in event planning but think you'd be great at it. You would like to find out more about her job but aren't sure how to ask.

The Possibilities
A) You corner her by the buffet and tell her why you think you would be a great event planner and why she should get you an interview at her company.

B) You have a chat about careers and then mingle with your other friends. You figure you aren't qualified for the position and aren't really looking, so why bother getting to know her.

C) You tell her you have always been interested in a career in event planning. You ask if she would be willing to talk to you some more about her job and ask if you can e-mail her to set up a better time.

D) You tell your friend to tell her you're interested in finding out about her job. You have him ask her to call you.

Your Solution
Choose the solution that you think will be most effective and write a few sentences explaining your opinion.
Then check your answer with the answer on our Web site: **www.mhhe.com/pace.**

Use Your Network

Your network is a very important tool to use when searching for work. The people in your network know you and can put in a good word for you. They also will know about job openings before they are offered to the general public.

A network also can help you trade information, goods, and services. Networking with people who work in your career field can help you with information about changing trends. Your friend at EXCorp knows where to get low-cost, high-quality office supplies, which will save your company money and show that you are a person with resources. If someone in your network needs a reliable plumber, you may happen to have the name of a reliable plumber.

Keep your network active. You never know when a dinner conversation can lead to a new opportunity. Also, remember to give as well as take from your network.

Getting in the Door: The Informational Interview

When you are first deciding upon a career or looking for a new job, consider researching it through an informational interview. The **informational interview** is a way for you to get information about your career from someone already in the field. It is also another way to build your network. The informational interview is not an interview for a job and should never be used as one. In this interview, you are the interviewer.

To begin, list the names of people in the career field that interests you. Use your network to target people. When you have a list, contact your targets either by telephone, mail, or e-mail. Explain that you are interested in their career field and would like to talk to them about career information and advice. Ask for 20 to 30 minutes of their time and find out where they would prefer to meet. You also may offer to do the interview over the telephone, but it's best to meet in person.

Preparing for the Informational Interview

To prepare for your interview, you should know something about the interviewee's field, company, and career. You want to be able to ask intelligent questions. Do your own research first and don't ask questions that you can find out on your own. Write your questions down. Then try to find the answers through books, in company literature, and on the Internet. The following questions will get you started:

- How did you get into the profession?
- What degree or training is needed for a job in this career field?
- What kind of preparation would you suggest for someone interested in this field?
- What are your major duties and responsibilities?
- What do you like most/least about your job?
- How long is a typical workweek for you?
- What skills and abilities do you find to be important in your work?
- What are some of the problems you face when trying to accomplish your goals?
- Is there a demand for employees in this career field?
- What are the salary ranges for the different levels in this career field?
- Do you have any special advice for anyone interested in this career field?
- Could you suggest anyone else for me to speak with in this career field?

Dr. Joe Pace
COLD CALL

Keep in touch with your network. No one likes it if you call only when you want something. Make an effort to stay in touch when you are not networking. Catch up for coffee, send holiday cards, remember birthdays, or send congratulations if you hear about promotions or job changes.

informational interview a way for you to get information about your career from someone already in the field

Conducting Your Interview

Arrive 5 to 10 minutes early on the day of the meeting. Remember to dress professionally and use your best manners. Keep your list of questions handy and be ready to jot down answers. Bring several copies of your résumé in case your interviewee would like to forward a copy to someone else. Of course, the tables may turn and you may become the interviewee, so be prepared.

Arriving at the interview on time and fully prepared lets the interviewee know that you understand the value of his or her time. Keep the tone of the interview relaxed but businesslike. Projecting a professional image leaves a lasting impression on your interviewee. That image may come to mind when the interviewee needs someone of your skills in the future or knows someone in his or her network that has the need.

Completing the Interview

At the end of the interview, ask the interviewee for the names of other people who might serve as a resource. Ask for permission to use your interviewee's name when you contact the people he or she mentions. Your network has just gotten bigger. Remember to send a thank you note to the person you spoke with within two days of your meeting. Show your appreciation for his or her time. Write a sentence or two about what you learned from the interview. Record the person's name, the interview date, who referred you, and when you sent the thank you note in your networking journal.

Using the Internet to Network

Dr. Joe Pace
Assistant Assistance

Always be polite to administrative assistants and receptionists—on the phone and in person. If you are rude or unpleasant to them, they have the power to make sure you don't get a meeting with their boss. If they are especially helpful, they deserve a thank-you note.

Because time is so valuable, some people may be more willing to communicate with you electronically. Internet networking is more difficult and time-consuming because your main means of communication is through the written word of e-mail. Face-to-face contact and body language cannot help you here. You must communicate clearly, concisely, politely, and professionally. Use correct grammar, spelling, and punctuation. Most e-mail systems can be set up to spell-check your message before it is sent. Remember, as with anything in writing, it could come back to haunt you, so take care what you write.

Building an Internet Network

The upside of Internet networking is that you can network across the globe, allowing your network to become large very quickly. Don't spread yourself thin. Find about five people you can communicate with on a regular basis. When choosing people for your Internet network, ask yourself the following questions:

- What do I have to offer this person?
- Can I do something now or in the future for this person?
- Does this person need information? Can I help or do I know someone who can?
- Can I offer this person career help now or in the future? Can he or she do the same for me?

Remember, as with face-to-face networking, Internet networking is a give-and-take relationship. Contact the people in your Internet network at least once a month. Even e-mailing a relevant newsletter or professional link is a good way to stay in touch.

Web Sites Company, association, and hobby-related Web sites are a great place to start networking. Web sites are a way for companies, associations, and hobbyists to post information and reach people with the same interests. Many sites have a "Contact us" link or list the e-mail address of a contact person. Read the Web site first. Find out all the information you can. When you are ready to make contact, use this information to begin the conversation. Talk about your mutual interests (hobbies and associations) or about the company's current projects.

Keep your e-mail short and easy to read. People who post their contact address usually have someone screen their e-mail. Give the person time to receive and read your e-mail. Wait at least a week before sending a follow-up message.

Mailing Lists The **mailing lists,** or *listservs,* are private or public group e-mail discussions. Public mailing lists are stored on Usenet. Private mailing lists are not. There are currently close to 100,000 mailing lists devoted to scholarly and professional topics as well as interests and hobbies. To use a mailing list, all you need to do is subscribe. To find a mailing list, use a list search engine. If you can't find a site you are interested in, start your own!

mailing lists also called *listservs;* private or public group e-mail discussions

Discussion Groups Discussion groups, or *Usenet,* are public online groups where you can discuss a topic. Many thousands exist on many topics. If you can't find a topic that interests you, start your own. An advantage to discussion groups is that you can find many experts on a topic very easily. A disadvantage is that your discussion is public and will be seen by many people. Usenet users are expected to know the social rules before entering a discussion. Experts suggest that you visit a site that specializes in discussion group etiquette.

discussion groups also called *Usenet;* public online groups where you can discuss a topic

Online Courses Online courses, or *virtual college,* are college-level distance learning courses offered online. About 250 colleges and universities offer online courses and degrees. Use the search engine of your choice and type in "distance learning" to find out more. Online courses have the advantage of putting you in contact with others in the same career field. Your virtual classmates can add much to your Internet network.

online courses also called *virtual college;* university/college-level distance learning courses offered online

QUICK RECAP 1.4

NETWORKING

Now you should have a better idea of the benefits and importance of networking. Here is a quick summary.

- A network consists of people you know. The people in your network have a network of their own.
- Networks are based on a relationship of give and take.
- A network is an important tool for finding work or information.
- An informational interview helps you gain knowledge of your career field. It is also an important networking tool.
- Being well prepared for an informational interview leaves a lasting impression on your interviewee.
- Internet networking can be difficult and time-consuming because the written word is your main means of contact. The upside is that your Internet network boundaries are now global.

CHECK YOURSELF

1. Name five sources you can use to build your network.
2. How can an informational interview help you?

Check your answers online at **www.mhhe.com/pace.**

BUSINESS VOCABULARY

informational interview   a way for you to get information about your career from someone already in the field

mailing lists   also called *listservs;* private or public group e-mail discussions

discussion groups   also called *Usenet;* public online groups where you can discuss a topic

online courses   also called *virtual college;* university/college-level distance learning courses offered online

Interviewing with Confidence

Today's job market is ever changing. Gone are the days when you worked for a single company until retirement. You could throw away your résumé and forget about ever interviewing with a stranger again. Employees today can expect to change jobs at least four times during their career.

So Nice To Meet You.   Interviewing has become an art. Successful people use the interview to sell their skills and accomplishments. They know how to open doors that are closed to others. Learn this art and use it to your best advantage.

Presenting Yourself at an Interview

An interview is your only time to make a good first impression. Making a good first impression involves dressing professionally and showing confidence—confidence you gained when you prepared yourself for the interview.

> **Reading and Study Tip**
>
> *Bulleted Lists*
> Scan the bulleted lists in this section. Create a short descriptive title for each list.

Types of Interviews

There are eight types of interviews: screening, one-to-one, committee, group, stress, unstructured, behavioral, and situational. Interviews can be initiated by you or by a prospective employer. They may last only 15 minutes or they may last an entire day. The interviewer may or may not tell you what kind of interview it will be. Try to find out beforehand if you can.

Screening Interview   The **screening interview** is a chance for the employer to see if you have the skills and qualifications necessary for the job. This type of interview generally is given over the telephone, so your best communication skills will be needed. Keep your answers short and to the point. Avoid giving away too much information.

screening interview a chance for the employer to see if you have the skills and qualifications for the job

One-to-One Interview   In the **one-to-one interview**, only one person interviews you. This person wants to see how your skills and experience can be of benefit to his or her company. It is one of the most common types of interview.

one-to-one interview a prospective employee is interviewed by only one person

Committee Interview   A group of people interview one person in the **committee interview.** This type of interview also can be a stress interview (see below). In a job with high stress levels, the employer wants to test your reactions to stressful events. The committee interview also may be used to see how well you can interact with several people at one time. It is becoming a popular way for companies to interview.

committee interview one person is interviewed by a group of people

Group Interview   A **group interview** involves several job hopefuls being interviewed by one or two interviewers at the same time. Employers use this type of interview when they are trying to find people with leadership and teamwork skills.

group interview several job hopefuls are interviewed by one or two interviewers at one time

stress interview uses a line of stressful questioning so the employer can evaluate how the interviewee handles stress

Stress Interview In the **stress interview,** the interviewer's job is to put you under stress and see how you react. This type of interview can be given in either the committee or one-to-one situation. You may be subjected to rapid-fire questions. You may receive curt comments or long periods of silence after you answer a question. The best way to handle this type of interview is to remain calm.

unstructured interview the interviewer asks one or two broad questions

Unstructured Interview The **unstructured interview** is a chance for you to show off your good communication skills and requires you to focus on how you fit the position. The interviewer will ask one or two broad questions, such as "Tell me about yourself" or "Tell me why you want to work for the NNN Company."

behavioral interview uses a line of questioning that seeks to find out how you reacted in the past

Behavioral Interview The **behavioral interview** uses a line of questioning that seeks to find out how you reacted in the past to certain situations. The idea is that past behavior is an indication of future behavior. "Tell me about a time when you had to work in a team." "Have you ever had to do more work than you could handle? What did you do about it?"

situational interview similar to a behavioral interview, except you are asked to describe how you would handle a situation

Situational Interview The **situational interview** is similar to the behavioral interview only you are asked to tell how you *would* handle a situation. "How would you deal with an employee who is consistently late to work?" "If you caught another employee stealing office supplies, how would you handle the situation?"

Making the First Impression

You never get a second chance to make a good first impression. The way you present yourself to the interviewer will determine whether or not you will be considered for the position. There are several things you can do: arrive early, dress professionally, sell yourself, and show self-confidence.

Plan to arrive at your interview at least 15 minutes early. Allow time for traffic and construction. Use the extra time to check your appearance in the restroom. Arriving late does not make a good impression. If you must be late because of an accident, for example, be sure to call your interviewer and let him or her know that you will be late and when you plan to arrive. How you dress and groom can help you make a positive impression. See Section 1.4 for tips on professional dress.

> ❝ *Self-confidence is so relaxing. There is no strain or stress when one is self-confident. Our lack of self-confidence comes from trying to be someone we aren't.* ❞
>
> *Anne Wilson Schaef*
> *Writer and Lecturer*

Strategies for Successful Interviews

Successful interviewees prepare for every interview as if it's their only interview. They develop a system and stick to it. The following strategies may help you.

Scheduling the Interview

Be courteous, professional, and clear with the interviewer or scheduler when scheduling on the telephone. This is one chance to make a good first impression.

Be sure that you have clear directions and know where to go in the building. Practice the route during the time of day you will be traveling to your interview. Check for construction, heavy traffic delays, and detours.

When scheduling several interviews in one day, overestimate on the time. Allow one hour for each. Make sure that you have allotted enough time for travel and preparation. It's best not to schedule too many for the same day.

If you have a choice about the time of day, schedule for the time when you'll be at your best. If you are going to be late for some reason, call ahead, apologize, and let the interviewer know when you expect to arrive. Make sure you arrive at that time. If this is inconvenient for the interviewer, ask to reschedule.

Research

All successful interviewers do their homework before they set foot in the building. In Section 1.1, you learned how to research a target company. Use those strategies to research the company with which you are about to interview. When you are well-informed about a company's structure, problems, and interests, you are better prepared to show how the company can benefit by hiring you.

While you're researching the company, you will also want to research the position for which you are applying. Your network may be able to help you discover this information. Also, a company's annual report can provide organizational charts. Some contain brief descriptions of the different departments and their functions.

- Is the position new?
- Why is the person in this position leaving the company?
- What kind of problems would you be asked to solve?
- What are the responsibilities of the position?
- Can someone in this position advance to a higher one?

Dr. Joe Pace
CHIT CHAT

Make small talk when you first meet your interviewer. If you see a picture you like in the office, say so. If you see golf clubs and you play, mention it. This shows you are personable and establishes a calm, friendly tone before the interview officially begins.

Tips From a Mentor

Questions to Answer When Researching a Company

- What does the company produce? What services does it provide?

- How large is the company? Has it expanded over the past five years or are people being laid off?

- Who are the company's major competitors and how do they view the company?

- Who are the customers and how do they view the company?

- Is the company doing well or is it having financial difficulties?

- Is the company privately or publicly owned?

- Is the company independent or is it part of a larger company?

- What are the company's most recent success stories?

- What problems is the company currently trying to solve?

- What is the culture of the company like?

- What is the rate of employee turnover? Is it high because of low wages?

- What is the interviewing and hiring process of this company?

Salary

Know what the position should pay before you interview but don't bring up the topic until the second or third interview. If the interviewer brings up the subject during the first interview, be prepared to discuss it.

To find out the high and low salary averages for a position, look to professional trade organizations and business magazines. They usually publish yearly salary surveys that offer information about position, level of experience, and geographic location. Keep in mind that salaries are based on the standard of living where the company is located. For example, a civil engineer in New York City may expect to make $50,077 at the low end and $57,680 at the high end. The same civil engineer in Mansfield, Ohio, can expect to make $38,849 at the low end and $46,559 at the high end.

What to Wear?

Choose what you will wear ahead of time and make sure that your clothes have been dry cleaned and pressed and are in good repair. Does your suit still fit well? Do you need to buy a new one? Check the condition of your shoes. Always err on the side of professionalism. This shows respect for your interviewer and helps make a good impression.

Practice

The list of goals, strengths, and weaknesses you made in Section 1.1 will help you prepare for some of the questions you may be asked. "What are your strengths and weaknesses?" "Tell me about yourself." "Why would you be right for the job?" "Where do you want to be in five years? Ten years?"

Other questions may test

- Your preparedness: "What did you do to prepare for this interview?"
- How well you work with others: "Tell me about a time when you worked as part of a team."
- Your weaknesses: "What are your reasons for leaving your current job?"
- Your work habits: "Are organizational skills one of your strengths?"
- Your time management: "When you experience heavy demands on your time, how do you prioritize tasks?"

Prepare your own questions to ask the interviewer. "How would you describe the work environment here?" "To whom would I report?" "Why is this position open?"

Practice interviewing with someone you know or videotape yourself if you can. Ask him or her for an honest opinion of your interviewing style. If you know the type of interview the company practices, focus on answering those types of questions.

What to Bring?

Plan ahead and put together the things you will need to take to your interview. Remember, these items need to fit inside your briefcase.

- Several copies of your résumé and list of references/reference letters.
- Your portfolio.
- A pad of paper and two professional-looking pens.
- List of interview questions for the interviewer.
- Telephone number for the company, in case you need to call while on the way.
- Tissues.
- An emergency kit, containing safety pins, breath mints/spray, a comb, a mirror, an extra tie for men, and extra hose for women.
- Business cards, if you have them.

Relax and Breathe

You've scheduled the interview, done your research, checked your interview clothes, practiced, and packed your briefcase. All you have to do now is relax and breathe. Allow yourself enough time to drive and to check your appearance before you meet your interviewer. A relaxed person projects confidence.

The Interview

Now you are ready for the interview.

- Greet the interviewer with a firm handshake, a smile, and direct eye contact. Use direct eye contact and smile naturally throughout the interview.
- Introduce yourself.
- Seat yourself when the interviewer invites you.
- Put your résumé directly into the interviewer's hands.
- Speak clearly and face the interviewer directly. Do not look away while either you or the interviewer is talking.
- Sell yourself. Expand on the information in your résumé. Talking about your accomplishments is not bragging. You have to show *why* you stand apart from all the others in line for the position.
- Give straightforward answers and statements.
- Never give a one-word answer, such as "yes" or "no." Explain why your answer is "yes" or "no." But beware of rambling—limit your answer to one minute or less. "Yes, I enjoyed the criminal procedure courses I took at the university. They gave me the opportunity to further my criminal justice credentials."
- Show your interest in the company. Use the information you found when researching. Interviewers want to know that the people who apply for positions know something about the company.
- Be honest and objective about your qualifications and why you left a previous position. Never speak negatively about former employers or companies.
- Stand your ground when faced with an aggressive interviewer. Answer his or her questions objectively and without emotion.
- Use gestures that are open and uplifting. Crossed or folded arms are seen as a protective gesture.
- Avoid pulling at your clothing, fidgeting, or tapping your feet. Keep your hands and feet relaxed.
- Never read materials on the interviewer's desk; such action is viewed as unprofessional and nosy.

Managing an Interview; Maintaining Control

Technically, the interviewer has the upper hand and holds the power during the interview. But sometimes the interviewer is inexperienced. He or she may tell you about the position and the company and forget to ask you necessary questions. He or she may begin to talk about something unrelated to the interview. Try to move carefully back to the interview. "If you don't mind, I'd like to share with you some of my experiences and how they relate to the job."

You also can gain and maintain control of an interview by answering questions in a way that reveals your agenda. Answer in ways that stress what you learned in your research about the company. Show how your skills and experience can benefit the company. Be careful not to overuse this method and take over the interview.

Another line of questioning can help you get a realistic picture of the job—things that the interviewer might want to hide about the position, such as high stress, frequent overtime, and excessive travel. "What is the turnover rate for this position?" "How much overtime is expected of someone in this position?" "How much traveling is required for this position?"

End It Well

Thank interviewers for meeting with you and tell them that you look forward to hearing from them. Always send a thank you note immediately after the interview.

The goal of a first interview is to get an offer that you can think about before moving to a second interview. Don't waste people's time if you are not seriously considering a position. However, don't immediately accept and say yes until you have gone home and had time to process what you found out and what you know.

Follow up with a telephone call if you don't hear from your interviewer within a week. If the decision process is still going on, ask when you might call back. Build a relationship with the employer that says you are interested. But beware of being a nuisance.

Negotiation Skills and Strategies

Talk of salary and benefit packages usually comes during the second or third interview. Some busy employers bring it up at the first interview in order to avoid wasting time with people who may be expecting too much. It's best to be prepared in all cases.

Before you go in for your interview, you should research the salary ranges for the position for which you are applying. When you have the knowledge of that all-powerful information, you are better prepared to approach salary negotiations. Here are some other strategies to help you:

1. Maintain a positive, professional, and polite attitude. Never use a "take-it-or-leave-it" attitude—you may end up with nothing. Show a "we-can-both-win" attitude.
2. Ask for a little more than you think the employer wants to offer. Then, you can negotiate a middle ground.
3. If the position has salary-grade restrictions, negotiate for other benefits, such as extra vacation days; flextime or a shorter work week; an early salary review; a one-time sign-on bonus; moving expenses; paid sick days; stock options; or additional medical, dental, eye, prescription, life, or disability insurance.
4. Be willing to walk away if your essential expectations are not met. Appearing desperate will allow the employer to get away with offering you less than top price.
5. Timing is very important. Wait until *after* the employer offers you the position to gain the most bargaining power. Let him or her name the salary first. Then go from there.
6. If you have received an offer from Company A, which offered a higher salary, but you would rather work for Company B, which is not offering a salary at that level, tell Company B that you have received an offer from Company A but would prefer to work for them. If you have done a good job of selling yourself, Company B will likely do its best to meet the other offer.
7. Reflect on the interview. Does the range offered fit your researched ranges? Does the range offered reflect the level of responsibilities mentioned in the interview?

Don't be too quick to accept an offer no matter how badly you want the job. Ask for a few days to think about it and tell your interviewer when you'll decide. Make contact when you say you will, even if you decline the offer.

Taking Rejection

You will probably not get a job the first time you send out your résumé. Likewise, you will probably not be offered a job at your first interview. It doesn't matter how impressed the interviewer seemed, you don't have the job until you sign the contract. It may help you to know in advance that you won't always be able to get your foot in the door. Don't take it personally or get discouraged. Boost your own self-confidence and keep trying.

QUICK RECAP 1.5

INTERVIEWING WITH CONFIDENCE

Now you should have a better idea of the benefits of knowing how to interview. Here is a quick summary.
- Presenting a professional and confident you at an interview makes a good first impression.
- Successful interviewees develop successful interviewing strategies and use them consistently.
- You can gain and maintain control of an interview by answering questions in a way that stresses your agenda.
- Come to the salary negotiation table armed with information and a positive, professional, and polite attitude.

CHECK YOURSELF

1. Name two strategies of successful interviewees.
2. What information is important to have during a salary negotiation?

Check your answers online at **www.mhhe.com/pace.** *Pace* ONLINE

BUSINESS VOCABULARY

behavioral interview   uses a line of questioning that seeks to find out how you reacted in the past
committee interview   one person is interviewed by a group of people
group interview   several job hopefuls are interviewed by one or two interviewers at one time
one-to-one interview   a prospective employee is interviewed by only one person
screening interview   a chance for the employer to see if you have the skills and qualifications for the job
situational interview   similar to a behavioral interview, except you are asked to describe how you would handle a situation
stress interview   uses a line of stressful questioning so the employer can evaluate how the interviewee handles stress
unstructured interview   the interviewer asks one or two broad questions

Chapter Summary

1.1 Researching Jobs and Careers

Objective: *Use online, personal, and local resources to begin your job search.*

In this section, you learned the importance of knowing yourself and setting goals for your career. You learned how to get practical about your goals, examining your needs and including your family in your plan. You used the Internet and other resources to research jobs.

1.2 Writing a Résumé

Objective: *Write a résumé that targets prospective employers.*

In this section, you learned that your résumé is your first chance to make a good impression. You learned that all résumés have the same basic structure but that there are several different types. You learned how to prepare an electronic résumé that you can post or submit online. You learned to begin with a generic résumé and to use your research in Section 1.1 to tailor your résumé for a specific position. You learned what to include and not to include in your résumé.

1.3 Promoting Yourself

Objective: *Use tools of professionalism, such as a career portfolio, to promote yourself in an interview and on the job.*

In this section, you learned that professionalism is revealed through what you wear, how you groom, how you use your

manners, and how you communicate. You learned what type of items should be included in your portfolio and when to present your portfolio during an interview. You also can use your portfolio during a performance review.

1.4 Networking

Objective: *Develop and use a network that helps you get your foot in the door.*

In this section, you saw that everyone has the beginnings of a network. You learned that networks are based on a relationship of give and take. You discovered the informational interview, how to prepare for one, and how it can help expand your professional network. You learned several ways to create an Internet network.

1.5 Interviewing with Confidence

Objective: *Conduct a successful interview that earns you a job offer.*

In this section, you learned that the interview is a chance to make a good first impression. It is a time to sell your skills and accomplishments. You discovered that there are eight types of interviews. You studied the strategies for giving a successful interview. You learned what it takes to manage the interview. You learned successful negotiation skills and strategies and how to use them to get a good salary.

Business Vocabulary

- behavioral interview (p. 32)
- chronological résumé (p. 14)
- combination résumé (p. 16)
- committee interview (p. 31)
- cost-of-living statistics (p. 5)
- discussion groups (p. 29)
- electronic résumé (p. 17)
- functional résumé (p. 15)
- goal (p. 4)
- group interview (p. 31)
- informational interview (p. 27)
- mailing lists (p. 29)
- network (p. 7)
- one-to-one interview (p. 31)
- online courses (p. 29)
- portfolio (p. 23)
- screening interview (p. 31)
- situational interview (p. 32)
- stress interview (p. 32)
- unstructured interview (p. 32)

Key Concept Review

1. What makes it easier for you to reach your career goals? (1.1)

2. Why is it important to keep a job search record? (1.1)

3. Why is it important to target your résumé to a specific company? (1.2)

4. Why is your résumé so important? (1.2)

5. What is a portfolio? (1.3)

6. Why is clear communication so important to professionals? (1.3)

7. How can a network help you in your job search? (1.4)

8. What is the significance of keeping a networking journal? (1.4)

9. Why should research be an important aspect of preparing for your interview? (1.5)

10. How can you manage and maintain control in an interview? (1.5)

Online Project

Showcasing Your Work

Many creative professionals use personal Web sites to showcase their work. Look for Web sites that function as online portfolios for photographers, artists, and graphic and Web designers. Use keywords like "design portfolio," "work" or "design samples", and "professional photographer picture gallery" to see what you can find. Choose the site that you think is the most professional and the best showcase for the creator's work, then share the address with your classmates.

Step up the Pace

CASE A   *Writing a Résumé*

You have been in the workforce for quite some time and are ready to start applying for jobs as a manager. You have decided it is time to write a complete professional résumé for yourself. You have so much information you don't really know where to start.

What to Do

1. Write your own history. Make three lists.
   a. For list one, outline your education from high school or GED to your most recent degree. List courses that earned you a certificate, qualification, or diploma. Include high grade point averages and accomplishments or honors.
   b. For list two, outline every paying job you have had and the dates of employment, from most recent to your first job.
   c. For list three, list any significant extracurricular activities in which you have been involved, any positions you've held, and your accomplishments in those positions.
2. Tell a story that shows your managerial skills. Show how one job led to another with greater responsibility, so that it is clear that you are ready to be a leader. Summarize the information on one page and then put it into a résumé format.

CASE B *Careers in Transition*

You are the receptionist at a local television station. A friend has been working as a personal assistant to a bank manager but wants to work in the entertainment industry. She wants your help getting into the business, but you aren't sure what you can do. You know she has no experience in TV, and, though you are friendly with all the people in a position to hire her, you aren't comfortable trying to set up an interview for her. You want to help your friend, but you don't want to put your colleagues on the spot.

What to Do

1. Discuss with your friend the skills required to do the different jobs in your company. Compare them with your friend's skills and interests. Find a match and then figure out who in your company holds that position.
2. Approach this person at your company during a quiet moment. Tell him or her about your friend, her skills, and her interests. Ask your colleague if he or she is willing to talk with your friend about his or her job responsibilities and offer her some advice about working in television. If your colleague agrees, ask for permission to give his or her e-mail address or phone number to your friend.
3. Give your friend the contact information and tell her that you have someone willing to meet her for an informational interview. Then leave the rest up to her.

Calculator Skills

No matter the field or department, almost everyone works with numbers at some time. A calculator is a helpful tool—as long as you input the numbers correctly. Use these tips when using a calculator:

- Use the + key to add, − to subtract, × or * to multiply, and ÷ or / to divide.

- Be careful which numbers you input first when subtracting and dividing (e.g., to find 5 − 1, input 5 first).

- Remember to round to the nearest cent when finding a money amount (for example, round $4.618 to $4.62).

- Press the = key to repeat a function. For example, instead of pressing 4 × 4 × 4 =, press 4 × 4 = =. Either way, the answer will be 64.

- To find a decimal number from a fraction, divide the top number by the bottom number. That is, to find the decimal equaling 1/4, input 1 ÷ 4 =. (Your answer should be .25 or 0.25)

- If a decimal repeats and repeats, round. For example, round 8.9999 to 9.

- The CE button clears only the last number input. C or Clear erases the entire equation.

- Many computers have a calculator function in them. Look under *Documents and Settings*.

- Use common sense when you look at an answer. If you get 5 for 25 × 5, you should know that the answer is not correct and you probably input the equation incorrectly.

Which is the correct way to input the following equation: 12 × 3 =?
Both C and D will compute the correct answer (36). The best way, however, is choice D.

Exercise: Use your calculator to find the answers for the problems below.

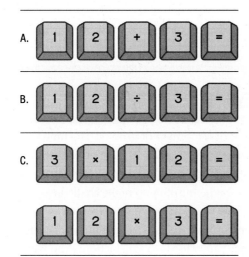

1. 63 + 98 =
2. 8 × 57 =
3. 2/5 =
4. 54 − 17 =
5. 185 − 66 =
6. 52 × 41 =
7. 3/4 =
8. 38 × 38 =
9. 3,482 − 1,978 =
10. 29 + 76 =
11. 50 ÷ 8 =
12. 649 + 533 =

At Work: Turning a Job into a Career

What Will You Do?

2.1 Setting Benchmarks Learn that making a plan and creating measurable steps are marks of successful professionals.

2.2 Recognizing and Seizing Opportunities Learn ways to work toward promotion and show your manager you're the person for the job; learn the benefits of building and maintaining an in-house network.

2.3 Broadening Knowledge and Skills Examine the reasons why successful professionals are constant learners; learn the dangers of not keeping yourself challenged.

2.4 Staying on the Right Track Learn to identify and avoid common career pitfalls; discover the difference between good and bad office politics.

2.5 Moving Up: Achieving Greater Influence and Respect Learn what it takes to develop and maintain a good working relationship with your manager; learn to distinguish between assertive and aggressive behavior.

Why It's Important

The word *career* suggests personal development or growth. The time you spend at work represents at least one-third of your day. Those thirds add up over the course of your lifetime! Wouldn't it be best to spend that much time doing something you enjoy—something you planned? Wouldn't it be fulfilling to make challenges for yourself, then work to meet them?

The word *work,* on the other hand, suggests "I need money to use for something else." The need to work for money rarely leads to satisfaction. Who would want to spend one-third of his or her life working just to pay the bills? Or work at a high-paying job that is a constant source of misery.

Chapter Objectives

After completing this chapter, you will be able to:

• Take the steps that will help you reach your goals.

• Recognize and seize opportunities for advancement and promotion.

• Learn the importance of continual learning.

• Learn what to do to stay on track with your career goals.

• Learn what it takes to achieve greater influence.

Set the *Pace*

Your Career Goals Think about your goals. Write a list of your career goals. Remember to include your family in the plans.

• Where do you want to be in 5, 10, 15, and 20 years?
• What steps do you need to take in order to reach your goal?
• Will you need more education or training?

Activity When you finish listing your career goals, work in groups of two. Share your career plan with your partner. Offer honest suggestions and critique each other's plans.

In Chapter 1, you took the time to think about your goals, your strengths, and your weaknesses. You targeted employers in your career field and learned how to research companies and salaries. You created your résumé and learned how to interview.

Now What? What do you do now that you have the job? How do you plan to achieve your goals when you're just beginning and starting near the bottom of the ladder? Of course, you need to work hard. You tend to your career like a gardener does to his or her prize roses. If you look at your job as "just going to work" every day, then your job will be just that—a job and not a career.

Seeking Ways to Develop and Improve as a Professional

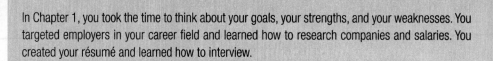
Reading and Study Tip

Ordering Words
When you give directions, you use order words such as *first, then, next,* and *finally.* You also use these words to describe the steps or stages in a process. Look for directions in this section. Write your own set of directions using order words.

benchmarks measurable steps that help you meet your goals

> ❝ *You hit home runs not by chance but by preparation.* ❞
>
> *Roger Maris*
> *Professional Baseball Player*

You know how to dress and groom properly, use correct manners, communicate clearly, and use proper posture. Now you're ready to become a professional, to show yourself worthy of your career and all it has to offer. First, you listen and look. How is your company organized? Who does what? Who makes the decisions? Who are the successful people? Who are the people you want in your network?

Next, you make a plan—write it down and keep it near. Your plan should include **benchmarks,** measurable steps that help you meet your goals. Where do you want to go within the company? What steps will you need to take to get there? Does this company meet your needs? Or will you need to move on to another company later in order to meet your goals? Will you need more skills training or education? Will your spouse want to move several states away when a dream opportunity opens up for you? Do you want to spend several hours a day commuting into the city? Use Figure 2.1 to help you plan your goals.

Then, you work to achieve your plan. Your plan may change at any time when your goals change. Be flexible when opportunity comes your way. But don't just take any opportunity. Ask yourself if this opportunity will help you step closer to your goals. You will need to evaluate your benchmarks and goals from time to time to see that they still meet your needs. Most professionals do this on a twice yearly or yearly basis.

Finding Balance

Successful professionals pay attention to all aspects of their lives: financial, social, health and fitness, and recreation. They try to strike a balance in their lives, both in and out of the office.

Figure 2.1 *Gail's Plan*

Gail's Plan	Goals	Benchmarks
1 year	• Be promoted to the surgical unit when position opens	• Volunteer for extra shifts in the intensive care or ER areas • Subscribe to several scholarly nursing publications • Create and maintain internal work network • Volunteer at community health fair
5 years	• Earn RN certification • Be promoted to head surgical nurse • Earn bachelor's degree	• Take evening classes while working during the day • Create and maintain a career network • Volunteer to organize the community health fair
10 years	• Be promoted to department head • Obtain Ph.D	• Take classes and do dissertation work in the evenings • Research consulting needs in the market • Work on possible client network

15 years	• Teach at the local university– moderate class load	• Teach 3 classes
		• Take additional business evening courses
		    –management –economics
		    –accounting –grant writing
		    –taxes
		• Create business plan for health-care consulting firm
		• Work on possible client network

20 years	• Start my own health-care consulting firm • Continue university teaching until the demands of business interfere	• Set aside at least 2 years' worth of savings • Set up home office or explore office space • Work on and maintain client network • Expand volunteer opportunities • Sponsor a booth at the community health fair

Thinking Critically Gail recently became a Licensed Practical Nurse (LPN). She works as a staff nurse at the local hospital but has other plans for where she wants to go. *How could Gail further define her benchmarks?*

Financial It's never too early to plan for the future. You need to think about your retirement and your child's education at the beginning of your career. Take the time to make a financial plan. Include it in your career plan. Here are some questions you need to ask yourself:

- Do I want to retire early?
- Do I want to buy a house?
- Will I pay for my children's education?

Then, you make your plan by setting specific goals. When will you need the money? How much will you need? Ask yourself the following questions:

- At what age do I want to retire?
- How much will a house cost? Where do I want to buy? When do I want to buy?
- When will my child be of college age? How much will his or her college education cost?

Internet Quest

Online Banking

Visit your bank's Web site. Search the site for savings options, retirement planning options, and investment options. Read the outline of each plan, looking up any information you don't understand. Choose a plan you think would help you meet your financial goals for the future. Write a brief paragraph about your choice and share it with the class.

401(k) a retirement plan to which both the employee and employer contribute

The next step is to get the money to meet those needs. Many employers have pension plans or **401(k)** plans for retirement. In a 401(k) plan, you can choose your investments and "grow" your own account. Some companies have savings plans, where you contribute a percentage of your wages while the company also makes a small contribution.

Outside of work, there are several other personal investment options. You can learn to play the stock market yourself and take charge of your own investments or get help from a financial planner. Handling your own investments can take a lot of time, but you can be more involved in watching your money. This can create stress for some people, especially when the market drops. A financial planner can help with your long-term goals. He or she also can give advice on employee benefits, investments, retirement accounts, insurance, and tax and estate planning.

Social   Well-balanced professionals make time for family, friends, and community. If your life is all about work, you have no time for social connections. These social connections affect your quality of life and are part of your all-important network.

Health and Fitness   Eating right and exercising are key for all humans who want to remain happy and healthy. You feel better about yourself, and more confident, when you are fit and healthy. It's easier to show your best professional self when you feel at your best. Take the time to fit exercise into your daily routine. Many companies have on-site fitness centers—take advantage of them!

Take scheduled breaks during your workday: sit down away from your desk and eat your meal or snack. When you take the time to plan for these breaks, you'll choose foods that are more healthful. Hurried breaks and lunches at your desk often mean that you'll stuff anything into your mouth without thinking and eat more of it than you really need. Time spent with co-workers at lunch and on breaks is quality networking time.

See your doctor, optometrist, and dentist for yearly and semi-yearly checkups.

> *You cannot afford to wait for perfect conditions. Goal-setting is often a matter of balancing timing against available resources. Opportunities are easily lost while waiting for perfect conditions.*
>
> *Gary Ryan Blair*
> *Author, Speaker, and Goal-oriented Strategist*

Recreation   Don't forget to relax and have fun. Recreation can include physical activities such as running, golfing, tennis, or mountain climbing. Recreation also can include hobbies such as cooking, knitting, collecting stamps, or restoring classic cars. Time spent doing the things you enjoy helps you relieve stress created by career and family demands. When you lower your stress level, you're much less likely to show unprofessional characteristics such as anger, frustration, or rudeness on the job.

Setting Career Goals within Your Current Job

The goals you set for your career are entirely up to you and depend on where and how far you can or want to go. Even if your current job cannot help with your career goals, conduct yourself like a professional. Use every opportunity to practice your professionalism now; when the right job comes along, you'll be ready.

Tips From a Mentor

Do's and Don'ts to Help You Reach Your Goals

- Do talk to people at work who can help you find out the present needs of the company. Make plans to fill those needs.

- Don't show a lack of interest in the company and your job by frequent absences or tardiness.

- Do expand your network of people inside and outside the company.

- Don't display rudeness, disrespect, or prejudice toward co-workers, customers, or other staff.

- Do volunteer to manage a project, teach new employees, write a proposal that fills a company need, substitute for your manager in a meeting, run a meeting, or assist with the budgeting process.

- Don't show unwillingness to meet deadlines, make decisions, or perform menial tasks.

- Do take every opportunity at work to learn a new technical skill or update your current skills to fill in gaps in your knowledge.

- Don't spend your time at work being lazy, surfing the Internet, or making personal calls.

- Do join an association, organization, or committee that will help with your long-term goals.

- Do talk to people in your current position at other companies and in positions you would like to work towards in order to find out what they did to move up the ladder.

QUICK RECAP 2.1

SETTING BENCHMARKS

Now you should have a better idea of the benefits and importance of setting benchmarks. Here is a quick summary:

- To achieve your goals, you must begin with a plan.
- To reach your goals, your plan should have measurable steps, or benchmarks, that help you get there.
- Successful professionals pay attention to all aspects of their lives.
- Even if your current job cannot help with your career goals, use it as an opportunity to practice your professionalism.

CHECK YOURSELF

1. What aspects of your life do you need to keep in balance?
2. List three actions that can keep you from reaching your goals.

Check your answers online at **www.mhhe.com/pace.**

BUSINESS VOCABULARY

benchmarks   measurable steps that help you meet your goals
401(k)   a retirement plan to which both the employee and employer contribute

Recognizing and Seizing Opportunities

You dress like a professional. You conduct yourself around co-workers and others like a professional. You are developing as a professional by making a plan for the future with measurable benchmarks. You are doing well at work, meeting the demands of your job. But it's often difficult to stand out from the rest of your co-workers when the company is large or your boss is a busy person.

Get Promoted. Chances for promotion may not come along very often. You want to be the person your manager thinks of first when a new position or opportunity opens.

Managing Your Manager

Rare is the company where you can still establish a long-term relationship and reputation with your manager. Managers change quickly in today's working world. Making sure that your manager knows your worth is more important than ever. It's just not enough to do a good job; your manager must *know* you did a good job.

Reminding your manager of your worth is easier once you've established a good relationship with him or her. Keep your manager informed on the progress of your projects. Write a report at the end of a project stating what went well and what could have been improved. Ask your manager for advice or feedback on a difficult task. Go over a copy of your agenda with your manager before going to meetings so he or she isn't caught off-guard. Keep the lines of communication open.

Working toward Promotion

Begin thinking about promotion the day you start your job. A **promotion** is a boost in position or job title. As soon as you learn your job and are comfortable with your knowledge, ask for more responsibilities or volunteer for more difficult projects. Be open to opportunities to cross-train in other areas. Don't forget to dress and to show your professionalism every day.

Tell Your Manager Why You're the Person for the Job

You have learned your job and are doing well. You communicate regularly with your manager. You have taken on more responsibilities. You have taken the time to cross-train in other areas. You dress well and show your professionalism. A new higher-level position has opened in your department. You know you are right for the job. What do you do?

In Chapter 1, you learned the importance of research and preparation. Research the salary ranges for similar positions (see Chapter 1). Knowing what the position is worth can help you establish your value and negotiate an appropriate salary.

If you need to interview for the position, get prepared. Take the time to write down specific examples of the things you have achieved in your current position. What did you do that was above and beyond your current duties? Give examples

---

Reading and Study Tips

Titles
When writing someone's job title, capitalize the first letter of every word, with the exception of articles such as *a, an,* and *the* and functional words such as *for* and *and.* Compare the format of the titles in each section header with job title examples. Notice if the same rules apply. On a separate sheet of paper, make up three fictional job titles for yourself using the rules for writing titles.

---

promotion a boost in position or job title

❝ *When one door closes, another opens; but we often look so long and so regretfully upon the closed door that we do not see the one which has opened for us.* ❞

Alexander Graham Bell
Scientist and Inventor of the Telephone

New Opportunities

Your Challenge

You have been working for the same company for a year under a manager you have never liked. You know that you do great work and have good ideas but feel that your manager has not given you opportunities to progress. You have a major personality conflict with your manager. Though you could have done more, you have always felt your boss ignored the efforts you made. You have just found out that your manager is leaving the company and will be replaced by a colleague you know well and respect. You have the feeling that this change could mean a great opportunity for you to finally start moving up. How do you take advantage of it?

The Possibilities

A. Just keep doing what you are doing, knowing that now that your buddy is the boss, you will be handed all kinds of opportunities.

B. Congratulate your friend on the promotion and ask for some time to discuss your past performance and the possibilities for increasing your job responsibilities once he or she is settled in as the new manager.

C. March into your new manager's office and give him or her the full story about how terrible your last boss was, how you never got the attention, respect, or money you deserve, and demand to be considered first for any promotion.

D. Invite your friend out to lunch and over to dinner at your house so you can use your friendship to your advantage.

Your Solution

Choose the solution that you think will be most effective and write a few sentences explaining your opinion. Then check your answer with the answer on our Web site: **www.mhhe.com/pace.**

❝ *Opportunity dances with those already on the dance floor.* ❞

H. J. Brown Jr.
Author

that can be measured. For example, ad deadlines were met with 17 percent greater efficiency than last year, or data entry errors in the department decreased by 5 percent over last quarter.

After you have your research information, set an appointment with your manager to talk about your interest in the new position. Make your request formally by stating your interest in the position and asking for a time when you could meet to talk about it. Use the interview tips you learned in Chapter 1. Be sure to show your manager why you're the right person for the job.

Understanding Job Titles

Job titles can vary from company to company. For example, a copyeditor in the business forms industry differs from a copyeditor in the publishing industry. A business forms copyeditor uses the customer's order, business forms specifications, and the knowledge he or she has of types of forms, inks, and papers to create a sample and a written specification for production. A publishing copyeditor takes the manuscript from the writer and reads and marks it for content, spelling, grammar, punctuation, consistency, and style.

Companies that use job titles usually file them, along with a job description, with the human resources (HR) department. Check with HR to see if you can access

Figure 2.2 *Sample Job Description*

Company: ABC Business Forms
Date: 1/05/2006
Job Title: Assistant Manager, Quality Control
Reports to: Manger, Quality Control
Salary: $34,000 to $48,000

Job Summary: The quality control assistant manager will inspect and monitor work and materials to ensure that established procedures are followed, to adjust procedures as needed, to advise, and to make recommendations to the quality control manager to ensure that all products meet established specifications.

Responsibilities: Monitor product quality in the production process. Inspect forms for proper location of text and rules. Check for proper spelling, punctuation, and grammar. Check that all production marks are properly located. Advise foremen of defective equipment and/or performance leading to poor quality. Recommend additional training when necessary. Interface between copyediting and prepress. Monitor and adjust procedures in production and copyediting.

Requirements: The quality control assistant manager must have an Associates or Bachelor's degree in English or Communications or 5 to 10 years' experience in the business forms industry. Must also have a good understanding of forms layout, font styles, and ruling placement; knowledge of manufacturing procedures, equipment, and materials used; an understanding of complex products and usage; good communication skills, written and verbal; functional knowledge of desktop publishing; and sound analytical skills. Must be competent in PC and basic software packages. Must be detail oriented, comfortable in a team environment, and able to handle pressure and deadlines. Note: if candidate lacks business forms certification, he or she must complete and pass the program before his or her one-year anniversary.

Thinking Critically This job description is for an assistant quality control manager at a business forms company. *What would the job description for your current position look like?*

this information. A **job description** will list a summary of the position, the responsibilities and skills needed in the position, a salary range, and the name of a supervisor. See the sample in Figure 2.2.

job description a summary of the position and its responsibilities

If your company does not use job titles or job descriptions, write your own. It will be a valuable exercise for you to examine the requirements of your job and the things you do every day. It's also a good thing to take to your performance review, especially if you are seeking a raise. You will be better able to show the work required to do your job.

In-House Networking and Team Building

Building relationships within your company can give you an edge over others when it comes to job security. The people with whom you network in your company can offer valuable information about new positions or openings, shifts in company policy, or changes that may affect your position.

Ten Tips to Help Build Your Office Network

- Go to lunch with different people on a regular basis and volunteer for projects that give you contact with other departments.

- Get to know people as individuals.

- Help others with a project or presentation by coaching, acting as a sounding board, or critiquing.

- Sincerely and formally thank people who have helped you.

- Acknowledge the contributions and accomplishments of others.

- Volunteer to help a co-worker or train a new person.

- Attend office parties and picnics and participate in office-sponsored volunteer projects.

- Show respect for the person who shares confidential information with you by keeping the secret. A trusted person gains the respect of others.

- Follow through on any promises you make. Nothing destroys a relationship faster than broken promises.

- Respectfully listen to and consider the advice given to you by others.

> ❝ Luck? I don't know anything about luck. I've never banked on it, and I'm afraid of people who do. Luck to me is something else: hard work—and realizing what is opportunity and what isn't. ❞
>
> *Lucille Ball*
> *Actress and Comedienne*

Being part of a team is another good means of networking. Team members have a network of their own. When you establish a good reputation as a team member, you have access to a much larger network. If your department does not work as a team, you can work to build a team that functions smoothly and gets things done.

Networking

Networking within your company is the same as networking outside. Take care that your networking doesn't become about using other people. Offer information, support, and help to those in your network and to those you want in your network. Build relationships based on give and take.

Using the Office Grapevine

Use the office grapevine with care. It can be a way to gain valuable information, but it also can be a vehicle for gossip and rumors. Don't participate in gossiping and spreading rumors; it can ruin the professional reputation you worked so hard to create.

Team Building

A few people working together for a common goal can accomplish more than 20 people working alone. Sports teams that work well together win championships; sports teams with outstanding individuals rarely make it to the final round.

Work seems a lot less like work when everyone is working toward a common goal. The workplace that doesn't function as a team is full of distrust, selfishness, and unhealthy competition. The workplace that functions as a team is more productive and efficient. The team uses time efficiently, comes up with better ideas, produces fewer errors, and makes for happier workers. Team members bring many skills, ideas, and information to the table.

Many companies require employees to work in a team environment. If your company fosters a team environment, use these tips to be a valuable team member:

- Show team members respect, trust, loyalty, courtesy, and professionalism.
- Listen to and be respectful of the opinions and ideas of others.
- Express your thoughts completely and in a professional manner to avoid miscommunication.
- Respect the diversity of the group.
- Be a role model for others in the team.
- Be flexible and open to change within the team.
- Include all members of the team in any and all communications about the team.
- Help new members get up to speed on projects.
- Share all information that affects the team with all members of the team.

If your company does not foster a team environment, work to build a team in your department. Develop goals and a plan. Tell your manager what you plan to do, how you propose to do it, and why a team environment would benefit the company. You never know where such an effort could lead. You may be asked to train other departments to set up teams of their own.

> **❝** *The sad truth is that opportunity doesn't knock twice. You can put things off until tomorrow but tomorrow may never come.* **❞**
>
> *Gloria Estefan*
> Cuban-American Singer and Musician

QUICK RECAP 2.2

RECOGNIZING AND SEIZING OPPORTUNITIES

Now you should have a better idea of the benefits and importance of recognizing and seizing opportunities on the job. Here is a quick summary:

- Reminding your manager of your worth is easier once you've established a good relationship with him or her.
- Begin thinking about promotion the day you start your job.
- Communicate regularly with your manager.
- Job titles and descriptions can vary from company to company.
- Building relationships within your company can give you an edge over others when it comes to job security.
- Offer information, support, and help to those in your in-house network and to those you want in your network.
- The workplace that functions as a team is more productive and efficient.

CHECK YOURSELF

1. Explain why research and preparation are important when applying for a promotion.
2. What are the dangers of using the office grapevine? What are the advantages?

Check your answers online at **www.mhhe.com/pace.**

BUSINESS VOCABULARY

job description   a summary of the position and its responsibilities
promotion   a boost in position or job title

Broadening Knowledge and Skills

Successful professionals are constant learners. When a barrier stands in the way of their goals, they find ways to get around it. Having many skills and a willingness to take on challenges will make you a more desirable and valued employee.

The School of Life. Continued education is essential for a professional. That doesn't mean you need to earn another degree, though. College may or may not be the place to learn new skills for your job. Seminars, conferences, or in-house training may be of more help. Experience is often the most valuable component of your education.

Taking on New Responsibilities

Once you have learned your job, ask to take on more responsibilities. Ask to be assigned one more project or to be **cross-trained** trained on another job, or in another department. Then, perform your new job well—meet the deadline or budget—and use your new knowledge. Success with more responsibility shows that you have strong organizational and time management skills.

Beware of taking on too much, too soon. Taking work home regularly and working excessive overtime leads to burnout and exhaustion, which shows that you are unable to manage your time efficiently or that you are disorganized. You may already have too many projects. If you try to take on even more, it shows that your need to get ahead is of more concern to you than the quality of your work.

Staying Flexible

Staying flexible can be a challenge in today's quickly changing workplace. Professionals in the fields of nursing/medicine, education, entertainment/media, and technology understand the value of flexibility. Inability to meet the demands of new information and technology can mean death for any rising career. Extremely popular and successful silent film stars who could not make the adjustment to talking pictures faded quickly from the public eye. Teachers and medical personnel who do not keep up with new information and technology find that their careers stagnate and that promotion is no longer an option for them. They find themselves merely working toward retirement.

Companies that need to reorganize and **downsize,** or cut their workforce because of financial difficulties, want to keep the workers who have the most to offer. Do the skills of Employee A meet the needs of the new Organization B? A cross-trained and skilled employee has the flexibility of moving from a soon-to-be-closed department to a newly formed department.

Sometimes a company needs to move or needs to move you to another location. Are you willing to move and restart your life? Refusing to do so can cost you your job in some cases. At the very least, your potential with the company could be limited. On the other hand, moving could be good for your career, expand your network, and offer new opportunities for you to reach your goals.

Reading and Study Tip

Flash Cards
Write the business vocabulary words in this section on note cards. Write the word on one side and its definition on the reverse. Have a friend quiz you on the words by showing you the card with the word side facing you. Once you know these words, make flash cards for the vocabulary words in the rest of the chapter.

cross-trained trained on another job

    Ah, mastery ... what a profoundly satisfying feeling when one finally gets on top of a new set of skills ... and then sees the light under the new door those skills can open, even as another door is closing.

        Gail Sheehy
        Author and Journalist

downsize cut a workforce because of financial difficulties

Continue Learning and Developing New Skills

The two most obvious ways to continue learning are training at your workplace and taking classes at a local university or college. Continuing your education beyond your current level says a lot about you as a professional. Knowledgeable workers are valuable workers.

Another way to continue learning is to attend training classes, seminars, and conferences related to your field. Some companies offer onsite seminars as well as on-line training courses. Courses and seminars include subjects such as computer and design programs, business and management skills, workplace safety, e-business, and project management.

You also can read and learn on your own. Look for books, industry journals, and business and leadership documents. If you're too busy to do a lot of reading, subscribe to an abstract service. **Abstract services** read the latest books and articles for you and give you a summary of the content.

abstract services read the latest books and articles and give a summary of the content

Company-Sponsored Education

Many companies will pay or help pay for business-related seminars and conferences or any further education you choose to pursue. Some companies even pay for job-related college courses or degrees. Check with your HR department. Here are some areas where you can concentrate on further education:

- Learn another language, such as Spanish, French, or Japanese. Learning another language shows that you understand the importance of the global marketplace.
- Learn how to use the most current technology, such as computer software, and the technology of your career field. Companies that step into the future need employees who can keep up with them.
- Learn positive negotiation and conflict resolution skills. The person who can respond to conflict positively and constructively earns the admiration and trust of co-workers and management alike.
- Learn leadership or management skills. College courses and on-the-job training rarely include the subjects of leadership and management skills, but you can find classes on them elsewhere.

The Dangers of Complacency and Comfort

Day-to-day work, family, and social obligations can cause even the most motivated of us to become **complacent,** or satisfied with things as they are. We become too comfortable and lose sight of our goals. We tell ourselves that we'll take that class next time or read those professional articles tomorrow. We say that we don't know a manager well enough to ask about a new position in her department.

The main danger of becoming complacent and comfortable is you may forget to take risks that can lead to success. Goals are cast aside and easily forgotten. Instead of being on the career track, we find ourselves on the track to nowhere.

complacent satisfied with things as they are

Dr. Joe Pace
RISKS

"If you always do what you've always done, you'll always get what you've always gotten."

Keeping Yourself Challenged

Risk involves challenging yourself to ask for that raise or promotion, pursue that interview with your dream company, or take that class in statistics. Success requires

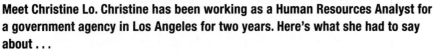

New Attitudes / New Opportunities

Meet Christine Lo. Christine has been working as a Human Resources Analyst for a government agency in Los Angeles for two years. Here's what she had to say about . . .

What She Does as a Human Resources Analyst. "What I do is job classifications and salaries. I study everything involved in a particular job: responsibilities, tasks, equipment used, etc. Then, I recommend whether a person's salary or title should be lower or higher."

The Biggest Mistake People Make in Terms of Developing a Career. "A lot of people just shoot for what they think they should be. They may have experience or skills appropriate for another job, but they don't *feel* qualified. They hear a title, like research analyst, and they think, "I don't have any experience in research." Most people think that I needed a science degree to do this job; but I have an English degree. At first, it might have helped me to have knowledge or a background in the area, but my employer gave me a lot of training. So you never know what job you can do!"

Staying on Top of your Career. "Try to learn more—not just about what you are trained to do for your job. Discover how work flows through your office, study your industry, research different departments, learn how to do your job on the computer. If you receive an assignment, find out where it comes from; or if you send your work on, find out where it goes and what that department does. Network, read, and ask."

What You Can Do if You've Been Laid Off or Fear Your Job Will Become Obsolete. "Don't be afraid to apply for different positions or in different departments. Have the attitude that, although your position's gone, you have knowledge that may be useful elsewhere in a company. That's where all that networking comes in. For example, if you're talking to someone doing something totally different, always find that commonality in what they do and what you do. Don't be afraid to apply in another department. So many people think, 'I'm under-qualified' or 'I don't know enough about that department.' Focus on the similarities. Keep networking and don't ever think that you're not qualified. If you don't get it, no one will blame you for trying."

some amount of risk. Be sure that you assess any and all risks you take. It's always a good idea to make a list of the positive aspects of the risk on one side and the negative aspects on the other. Here are some questions you should ask yourself:

- Does this risk get me closer to my goals?
- What is involved in this risk?
- Is the risk worth the effort?
- What is my potential gain and what is my potential loss?
- Is the risk consistent with my beliefs and morals?
- How will my family be affected?
- Can I live with the results?

Sink or Swim

Another danger with complacency is that you can be left behind or left out when your skills become outdated. In today's business world, companies are bought and sold as quickly as one changes one's mind. Larger, more technologically advanced companies buy smaller, less technologically advanced companies.

Figure 2.3 *You Be the Judge*

Mario's Approach	Luis' Approach
Dresses professionally	Dresses unprofessionally
Loves his job	Likes his job
Reads industry magazines and books	Reads the newspaper
Learned how to use the computer as a tool	Does not want to use the computer much
Attends business school	Does not want to take classes
Asks for advice from an experienced buyer	Avoids "higher-ups"
Spends his own time getting to know the company and the job	Doesn't want to spend any more time thinking about the company or the job

Thinking Critically Although both men want to be a senior buyer, only one is likely to get the job. *What could Luis do to get back on track with his goals?*

Whether or not you weather the storm of layoffs and firings will depend largely on your usefulness to the takeover company. It will not matter if you've been with the company for many years. You will be evaluated as either an asset or a liability, depending on the value of your skills, experience, and education. Any company that has just spent millions of dollars for another company will try to combine all assets and eliminate as many liabilities as possible. The decision will be about how you affect company profits. (See Figure 2.3.)

QUICK RECAP 2.3

BROADENING KNOWLEDGE AND SKILLS

Now you should have a better idea of the benefits and importance of broadening your knowledge and skills. Here is a quick summary:
- After you have learned your job, you should begin asking to take on more responsibilities.
- Professionals understand the value of flexibility.
- Continuing your education beyond your current level says a lot about you as a professional.
- The main danger of complacency and comfort is that you may forget to take risks that can lead to success.
- You can be left behind or left out when your skills become outdated.

CHECK YOURSELF

1. What are the dangers of taking on too much responsibility at the beginning of a new job?
2. Name three ways to continue your education.

Check your answers online at **www.mhhe.com/pace.**

BUSINESS VOCABULARY

abstract services   read the latest books and articles and give a summary of the content
complacent   satisfied with things as they are
cross-trained   trained on another job
downsize   cut a workforce because of financial difficulties

Staying on the Right Track

In the previous section, you learned that continually working on your personal skills and knowledge can help you achieve your goals and make you a valued asset. This section will deal with what you can do on the job to help you achieve your goals. What you do on the job is at least as important as how you prepare for your job. What you do on the job will determine whether you'll be considered for promotion to positions of leadership.

Avoiding Career Pitfalls. To continue moving upward in your career, you need to recognize actions that will slow you down or stop you. How you handle mistakes can make all the difference in how much damage is actually done—both to the company and to your career.

Reading and Study Tips

Tables

Tables are a way to organize information. Look for tables in this section. How do they help you find information more easily? Find one heading containing information you think could be made into a table. Draw that table on a separate sheet of paper.

Pitfalls You Already Know

Everyday there are many opportunities to make mistakes. Learn what to do and what not to do. You have already read about some actions that can throw you "off track," including

- **Not having a plan.** When you don't have a plan to reach your goals, you can waste time on activities that won't get you any closer to your goal.
- **Lacking flexibility.** You have to be willing to depart from your plan should a new opportunity send you in another direction.
- **Not furthering your education.** Show your willingness to educate yourself and show your awareness of trends and new technology in your field.
- **Remaining silent about deeds.** Don't remain silent about the good things you have done; mention them to your manager when you have the opportunity.
- **Deciding to risk or not to risk.** Successful people are willing to take reasonable risks to avoid becoming outdated. Taking unreasonable risks can damage your reputation and career.

More Pitfalls

Many people don't realize how much their own attitudes and actions can hurt them. Some actions give the impression a person is a bad worker. Others give the impression that someone is actually a bad person. Examine your own actions and how others react to you. Have you fallen into any of these traps?

Showing Your Dark Side

Bad impressions can do great damage and are usually more permanent in the minds of others than any good works you do. Show your best professional side in company meetings, meetings with customers and vendors, social events, and interactions with your co-workers. Do you appear arrogant? Do you talk too loud, too fast, or too soft? Do you talk too little or too much? Does your body language show a lack of confidence?

Here are some other characteristics that show your dark side:

- **Trying to control everything.** Although some control over our lives and the people around us is necessary, too much control can damage your career. People who feel controlled are less willing to work for you. You'll look more like a manipulator than a person who can get things done. Try to influence people instead of controlling them. Building trust and loyalty is the best way to influence people.
- **Being obsessive about tasks or projects.** Of course, it's a good idea to want to do a good job, make a deadline, and achieve, but going too far is a sure way to make enemies. Often, today's companies value flexibility over the ability to meet deadlines. Be willing to ask for help, amended deadlines, or additional resources. Be willing to admit that you underestimated the demands of a project.
- **Bringing your personal life into the workplace.** Negative things such as personal, financial, and family problems can affect your mood, work performance, and work or business relationships. Even positive things, such as talking about your children's accomplishments or planning your wedding while on the job, can distract you from your work and annoy others.

Limited Identification

Being known for only one project or skill is a danger to any rising career. Let others see that there is more to you than one shining moment. It is also dangerous to become identified with one particular group of people who hang around together. The poor reputation or behavior of one group member can spoil the reputations of others. Socializing with one group also limits your in-house networking opportunities.

Poor Time Management

Poor time management is sure to keep you from being promoted. People who are unable to manage their time properly frequently miss deadlines, work an excessive number of hours, and often find themselves the victim of burnout. Here are some signs of poor time management:

- Spends more time setting up a project than is needed to do the project itself.
- Frequently misses deadlines and offers several excuses why.
- Procrastinates until the last minute and turns in sloppy, quickly done work.
- Does personal business on company time, such as making personal calls or paying bills.
- Arrives to work late and leaves early.
- Takes long lunches and breaks.
- Visits excessively with co-workers.

Making a List One of the most effective time management tools is making a list. Take several minutes at the beginning of each day to list the tasks you need to accomplish. Some professionals create lists for weeks and months to come. When working on a team project with a deadline, it helps to schedule the daily or weekly tasks at the beginning, so that all team members know what needs to be done and by when. For an example, see Figure 2.4.

Figure 2.4 *Managing Time*

Project: Silver Springs
Subject: Wastewater Improvement
Goal: Assess current situation and create a plan for improvement
Start Date: September 1, 2006   **End Date:** September 15, 2006
Budget: $52,000
Schedule:

September

1	8:00	Team mtg.: Discuss project, make a plan, assign tasks.
2	8:00	Team mtg.: Begin work: Team visits treatment plant; takes samples at source, at intake, during process, and at out-take; interviews plant manager; and reviews plant and process procedures.
3	8:00	Team mtg.: Review info from mgr. Create telephone survey for residents (Keith, Karen, Tye), begin testing (Leon, Masuto, Conrad), begin research (Leslie, Toni, Fredo).
4	8:00	Team mtg.: Review survey questions. Begin survey (Keith, Karen, Tye). Continue research and testing.
5		Continue survey, research, testing. Department meeting 2:00: Report on progress (Masuto, Karen, Fredo).
8	8:00	Team mtg.: Review progress of testing, research, survey. Compile survey results (Keith, Karen, Tye).
9	8:00	Team mtg.: Review survey results; research and test results due.
10	8:00	Team mtg.: Prepare report of results, research, and testing.
11	8:00	Team mtg.: Reports due; prepare presentation; practice.
12	8:00	Team mtg.: Present to department mgr.; make adjustments.
15	8:00	Team mtg.: Present to City Council.

Thinking Critically The team working on the Silver Springs Wastewater project worked out a schedule everyone could live with. *How different would the schedule look if it were created for just one individual on the team?*

prioritize to order a task according to each respective task's relative importance

Setting Priorities After you have made your list, prioritize your tasks. To **prioritize** means to decide which tasks need to be done first, next, and so on. To decide which tasks need to be done first, ask yourself: How important is this task? When does it need to be accomplished? How long will it take?

Meetings Meetings can eat up a major chunk of your time. Spend as little time as possible in meetings that have little to do with you. For large meetings that will take most of the day, make arrangements with the meeting manager to be called when you are scheduled to appear on the agenda. Ask to be excused after doing your part unless there is a good reason for you to stay.

multitasking doing more than one thing at a time

Multitasking Multitasking—doing multiple things at once—is another way to manage time effectively. Seek ways to reduce repetitive tasks, such as handwriting the same information on forms. Re-create the form on your computer with the repetitive information already filled in. Then, you only need to add the new information. You can print out a neatly written form. Save the document so you'll also have a non-paper record for future use.

Abusing the Internet or E-mail

At work, e-mail should be used for business purposes only. Have your friends send personal e-mails to your home. Ask others not to forward jokes and stories, which take up memory and take up time to download. Create a set time for checking e-mail rather than wasting time constantly checking your messages.

Do not visit inappropriate or unprofessional Web sites at work. Many companies periodically monitor Internet use by their employees. It could be embarrassing and career-damaging to be found on certain sites.

Burnout

Burnout is a trap that can damage your health as well as your career. Employees and co-workers with burnout often suffer from illness, lack of enthusiasm, quick or un-justified anger, and lack of patience and tolerance. Working excessive overtime during the week and taking work home on the weekends will most surely lead to burnout. Burnout occurs when the stresses are stronger than the rewards. Sometimes we bring burnout on ourselves by wanting to please everyone. Or we burn out because we are ineffective managers of our time.

To avoid burnout, learn to manage your time effectively. Say no when you need to say it. Avoid taking on more work than you can handle. It looks much better for you when you can finish a few projects on time and correctly than it does if you volunteer for everything and never finish anything.

Avoid Office Intrigues and Bad Politics

Becoming involved in office intrigues and bad politics, such as hurtful gossip, can damage your credibility and reputation. Gossip gives the impression that you have nothing better to do, that you are jealous and malicious, and that you are willing to associate yourself with hurtful lies.

Office intrigues and bad politics are not limited to gossip. They can include in-appropriate humor or comments that demean the race, nationality, gender, religion, or age group of another person. They can include talking negatively about the company, a project, a client or vendor, management, another department, staff members, co-workers, or team members. They also can include cruel practical jokes and efforts to exclude people from important information, such as meeting times/places or other necessary information.

In order to avoid being associated with hurtful gossip and negative behavior, socialize with only the most professional people. It will be difficult to determine which of your colleagues is professional if you are new to the job. You'll need to keep your eyes and ears open. Start by associating with many groups of people. If the conversation in one group turns to hurtful gossip, excuse yourself politely. You don't have to exclude these people from your office life. Just let them know that you will not be a part of any hurtful gossip.

When you're the new person, many people are eager to offer advice on whom to trust. Listen carefully, but make your own assessments. People are often labeled unfairly.

Good Politics

Practicing good office politics requires developing good relationship skills. You learned in Section 2.2 that networking is a relationship of give and take. All good relationships are based on mutual respect and trust. When you deal evenly and fairly with everyone—friends and enemies alike—you pave your path for promotion. You become known as a person who can work with anyone to accomplish anything. Here are some ways you can build good political skills:

- Do what you say you will do. If you say that you will get back to someone, do so in a timely manner.
- Do not lie, postpone, pass the buck, or avoid a situation or person.
- Be consistent. Inconsistency leads to mistrust.
- Keep everyone who needs to know in the communications loop.
- Praise people often. Catch them doing something correctly.
- Say "please" and "thank you" often.
- Take people at face value. Put yourself in their shoes. When you refuse to position yourself as a judge of past or current deeds, you help create valuable allies.
- Do not waste people's time. Keep telephone calls, conversations, meetings, e-mails, and memos brief and to-the-point.
- Be on time to meetings, appointments, and training sessions.
- Be loyal to your team members, co-workers, staff, customers and vendors, other departments, management, and the company.
- Share your information and resources freely and fairly.

Never look back unless you are planning to go that way.

Anonymous

Moving On: Making a Lateral Move

lateral move a move from one position in a department to a similar position in another department

Making a **lateral move** means moving from one position in a department to a similar position in another department. Lateral moves can mean new opportunities, new skills, and new contacts. Moving to another department demonstrates your flexibility and adaptability. Before making the move, ask yourself if it will help you reach your goals. Will there be room for promotion and movement in the new department?

There are several reasons to make a lateral move:

- Your current department does not help you meet your goals.
- Your career goals change.
- Your current department is outdated and may be downsized or eliminated.
- There is no room for promotion or growth.
- Despite your best attempts at team building, the people in your department are unable to work together.

Dealing with Termination

Losing your job under any circumstances can be frightening and humiliating. People lose their jobs for several reasons: Their skills are outdated; they are unwilling to meet new challenges; they show unprofessional behavior; they are guilty of excessive absenteeism or tardiness; the company is having money problems and needs to downsize or lay off.

The way you exit a job can say a lot about you as a professional. You want to avoid burning any bridges. After all, you will want to use your in-house network

Moving On?

Your Challenge
You have been working for a shipping company that has been hurt by the economy. Everyone around the office says that it is only a matter of time before your company declares bankruptcy; layoffs are sure to follow if that happens. You have only been at the company a year. You have no seniority and no family to support, so you are sure you will be one of the first to go if the company starts downsizing. You are really scared at the prospect of losing your job, but you aren't sure what you can do.

The Possibilities
A. Quit your job immediately and take some time to relax, sleep in, watch TV, and unwind before the bills pile up and you have to look for a new job.

B. Just keep your head down, do your work, wait, and hope for the best.

C. Announce to everyone at work that you will be looking for a new job and that you don't care if you get laid off because the company obviously had been run into the ground by poor leadership and ignorant managers.

D. Update your résumé, start making discreet calls to people in your network, and begin researching new job opportunities. While still at work, try to make yourself as valuable and optimistic as possible in order to keep your options open.

Your Solution
Choose the solution that you think will be most effective and write a few sentences explaining your opinion. Then check your answer with the answer on our Web site: **www.mhhe.com/pace.**

---

contacts as references or as the machinery to help you find your next position. Here are some ways to deal with termination:

1. Don't panic, show your anger, or vent your frustration with your manager or co-workers.
2. Negotiate calmly and professionally for things like continued insurance coverage, severance pay, or career counseling.
3. Ask your family and friends for comfort and support.
4. Get plenty of rest, eat properly, and exercise. You will need to be your best for the round of interviews ahead.
5. Assess your skills. Do you need to upgrade or update? Is it time for a career change?
6. Objectively examine your attitude or behavior if you lost your job for that reason. What areas do you need to change or work on?
7. Put your network to work.

Moving On When You've Reached Your Growth Limit

When your current company can no longer help you meet your goals, it's time to move on to greener pastures. A **resignation** is a formal notification of your departure from the company. No matter what your reasons for leaving, try to remain on

> **Pace Points**
>
> **It's Not Personal**
> Don't let being laid off make you doubt yourself. These days, dismissals have less to do with an individual's performance and more to do with economic factors. A layoff is not a reflection of your skill or worth as an employee. Look at termination as a chance to move on to better things.

resignation a formal notification of departure from a company

Figure 2.5 *Sample Resignation Letter*

Dear Ms. Pennington,

Last week, I accepted a position with Travel.com, an Internet travel agency, as international data operations manager. This represents a major opportunity for me, as I will be relocating to Paris, France.

Please accept my resignation, effective June 30, 2004.
I will be happy to help you find and train a replacement for my position.

I appreciate T.K. Teksystem's investment in my career development. I have learned a great deal from you, Ms. Pennington, about data operations and management style. I will take this knowledge to my new position.

Sincerely,
Janet Kiefer
6/15/2004

Thinking Critically Notice that the tone of the letter is positive. *Why is it wise to thank a company for its investment in your career development?*

good terms with your employer because you will need references and you may want to work for the company again.

A resignation letter should contain a positive explanation for your resignation, the date of your resignation, and a thank you for the experience. This letter will become part of your permanent employment file. See Figure 2.5 for a sample resignation letter.

Resign Gracefully

After you have written your resignation letter, make an appointment with your immediate manager to hand it over. During your meeting, make it a point to indicate verbally that you enjoyed working with your manager and the company.

Some companies require an exit interview. If your experience was not positive, choose to dwell on your positive reasons for leaving: You want to further challenge yourself; you want to start your own business; it's time for a career change. Consider discussing your personal reasons for leaving, such as relationship problems with your manager or co-workers, or because you did not receive the recognition you thought you deserved. Some departments will put the information to good use, while others will use it to harm your reputation. Be especially careful if you still want a reference from the company.

Make sure that you give adequate notice of your leaving. Two-weeks' notice is usually standard. Check with your company handbook so see if your company requires a longer notice period. Make sure that all your work is up-to-date and your files and papers are clearly marked and well organized. Leave a list of instructions for doing your job, a list of what remains to be done, a list of names and numbers of people who can be resources for the new person, and some tips you learned along the way. Your replacement will remember you well for your thoughtfulness.

What to Do When You're Really Unhappy at Work

Tamika is a single mother with two teenage children, Marcus and Raylyn. She is unhappy with her current position as a receptionist at a family-owned electrical supply company in a rural area. Though she is currently working toward certification as an electrician, she has been passed up for promotion to the position of order fulfiller several times by family members of the owner. Tamika is bored and feels that she can go nowhere. She is unable to leave for a better opportunity because she shares custody of her two children with her ex-husband.

Many people find themselves in a situation similar to Tamika's. They are stuck in an area because of family circumstances. They work at a company where **nepotism,** or favoritism shown toward family members when granting jobs, is practiced. They have been passed over for promotion; suffer from burnout, boredom, and lack of opportunity; endure the effects of personality conflicts with managers or co-workers; or are in the wrong career.

nepotism favoritism shown toward family members when granting jobs

More Education   Tamika is doing one positive thing that will help her after her children graduate. She is getting training as an electrician. There are other things she can do to improve her position at work. When another position opens, Tamika can remind her boss that she is studying.

Build an Experience Base and Network   Tamika can gain more practical experience. During the week, Tamika is busy with work, school, and her active teens. During the week that her ex-husband has the kids, she has more time, especially on the weekend. She can use her network of contractors that come into the company to apply for part-time work. She knows that many contractors who come in complain that they have difficulty finding good workers. When she gains more experience as an electrician, she can apply for full-time work with one of them.

Research Options   Tamika can explore her options now, so she is ready when she can move to an area where there is opportunity. The time she spends now looking in-depth at her career, her goals, and the options ahead will make it easier for her to hit the ground running when the time comes. She can find out early if this is a career she really enjoys. Positive activities and something real to look forward to will help her fight boredom and burnout.

Solutions on the Job

To get ahead, you must find a way to overcome any obstacles. Use these strategies to help revitalize your work.

- Have an optimistic attitude. Negative thinking makes you feel powerless and keeps you from doing the things you need to do to better your situation.
- Seek out a therapist for help in dealing with personality conflicts or problems.
- Seek advice from a career counselor. He or she may be aware of options that you don't know about.

- Ask for a transfer to another department. Make certain that you are not running away from problems rather than looking for new experiences and skills.
- Swap jobs with another co-worker or team member for a few days or hours each week. Not only will you be learning new skills, you also will chase away boredom.
- Ask for a flexible schedule that helps you fit in the activities you need to improve your situation. For example, the only class you have to take to finish your degree meets at 8:00 A.M. You attend the morning class and work a full day afterwards.
- Ask to telecommute or telework. **Telecommuting** employees work at home part or all of the week instead of going to the office. **Teleworking** employees use telecommunications technology, such as the phone, a fax machine, and Internet access, to work outside of the office. Most teleworkers work away from the office one to three days a week.
- Form a work support group that meets regularly.
- Try team-building, especially if your department does not work as a team. Even good teams need a boost from time to time to revitalize team spirit. Search the Internet for organizations and companies that offer on-site team building and training. Convince your manager that the results will be worth the cost.
- Ask your manager for more specific coaching or supervision. You will get to know each other better. You'll become better acquainted with the goals of your manager, and he or she will become better acquainted with your work and your value to the company.

Seminars and conferences are a way to improve your work situation, as well as your personal situation. Your entire department can be revitalized by a seminar on team building or a conference on new technology in the field. Better still if you are the one who suggested the seminar or conference. It makes you look like someone who can solve problems well.

telecommuting employees work at home part or all of the week instead of working at the office

teleworking employees use telecommunications technology to work anywhere away from the office

---

QUICK RECAP 2.4

STAYING ON THE RIGHT TRACK

Now you should have a better idea of the benefits and importance of staying on the right track. Here is a quick summary:
- There are many opportunities to damage your career.
- Being involved in office intrigues and bad politics, such as hurtful gossip, can damage your credibility and reputation.
- If you are faced with termination, the way you exit a job can say a lot about you as a professional.
- When you leave a position for a better opportunity, work to remain on good terms with your employer; you will need references and you may want to work for the company again.
- People who are unhappy at work and are not able to change jobs have several options available to them for personal improvement and work environment improvement.

CHECK YOURSELF

1. Explain how mismanagement of time can lead to burnout.
2. Name six ways to practice good political skills.

BUSINESS VOCABULARY

lateral move   a move from one position in a department to a similar position in another department

multitasking   doing more than one thing at a time

nepotism   favoritism shown toward family members when granting jobs

prioritize   to order a task according to each respective task's relative importance

resignation   a formal notification of departure from a company

telecommuting   employees work at home part or all of the week instead of working at the office

teleworking   employees use telecommunications technology to work anywhere away from the office

Moving Up: Achieving Greater Influence and Respect

You've been on the job and are working hard and doing your best. Now, it's time to achieve a benchmark on your career plan: promotion. You know the structure of your company. You know where you want to go next. You are on the right track toward reaching your goal, but how do you get there when five other people in your department have the same goal? What will set you apart from the others?

Marked for Success. In Section 2.2, you learned some strategies for managing your manager. Here, you will learn in more detail how to build a relationship with your manager that will set you apart from others in your department also jockeying for position.

> *Don't sit down and wait for the opportunities to come; you have to get up and make them.*
>
> C. J. ("Madame") Walker
> *African-American Entrepreneur, Beauty Industry Businesswoman, and Social Activist*

Close the Gap between You and Your Supervisors

Most managers love to develop, or groom, the people who report to them. Allow your manager to constructively criticize you, coach you, go to bat for you, and mentor you. Allow your manager to take credit for your polished professionalism. It will look good for both of you. When your manager moves up, he or she will certainly recommend you as a potential replacement!

Communicate Often

Communicate often with your manager, and do it in the style he or she prefers. Notify your manager of a project that has been finished. Pass along important information.

If your manager prefers personal conversation, learn his or her schedule so that you can approach him or her when it's convenient. Make your conversation brief so as not to take too much time from your busy manager.

If your manager prefers written communication, make sure that your writing is clear and concise and free of errors in spelling, grammar, and punctuation. Write a report about a project that has just been finished. Write a note of congratulations to your manager for something he or she has achieved.

Know Your Manager's Goals

You're in a better position for promotion if you can speak intelligently about your manager's goals. Knowing the goals of your department and your company helps you to better help your manager. It shows that you understand the reason why things are done the way they are. You know why the unpleasant jobs, as well as the more enjoyable jobs, need to be done.

Many managers do a good job of communicating their goals for their respective departments. If your manager has not communicated this information, ask. He or she may need to think about your question and get back to you. Share what you learn with your team.

Performance Reviews

Ask your manager for periodic performance reviews. Because you allow your manager to coach you, he or she will willingly acknowledge your professional development. Be sure to ask for suggestions on how to improve.

Be Well Informed

Nothing will impress your manager more than showing that you are well informed. Read the same magazines, journals, and books as your manager. Study and read your company's annual report. Slip the knowledge you gained into your conversations with your manager.

The Professional Employee

The way you conduct yourself with your manager can say a lot about your fitness for promotion. The person who shows professionalism every minute of every day tells those in charge that he or she can represent the company with dignity and respect. Here are some tips for the professional employee:

1. Behave well in meetings: arrive early, take notes, listen respectfully, turn off your cell phone or pager.
2. Offer to do things before you are asked to do them—even the unpleasant tasks. This shows that you are a can-do, take-charge kind of person.
3. Never make your manager look bad in front of others. Professionals treat those who outrank them with respect and dignity.
4. Admit your mistakes quickly and ask for advice on how to do better next time.
5. Be a problem solver. People who show they are problem solvers make themselves indispensable to their manager.
6. Always tell the truth, but avoid being blunt or hurtful. Choose your words carefully.
7. Don't involve your manager in your personal life or problems.
8. Remember and acknowledge the dates, such as birthdays and anniversaries, that are important to your manager.
9. Don't waste your manager's time. Even though he or she may be willing to mentor you, this doesn't mean that you should go to him or her for help with trivial problems.
10. Make your manager look good. When he or she moves up, you are in a better position to move up as well.
11. Say "Thank you" often.

Make Your Opinion Matter

Making your opinion matter comes from building a reputation of respect and trust. When you do your homework and are able to speak knowledgeably about your field, you gain the trust and respect of those who outrank you. When you learn how to take reasonable risks that have a good outcome, others will trust your advice and opinions. Others will look to you for possible solutions to tough problems.

Treat everyone you come in contact with in your office with respect and dignity. That includes the janitorial staff, the security staff, and the administrative staff. Staff people can have a strong influence on those in power.

> *The more you seek security, the less of it you have. But the more you seek opportunity, the more likely it is that you will achieve the security that you desire.*
>
> **Brian Tracy**
> *Author, Speaker, and Consultant on Personal and Professional Success*

> *No person who is enthusiastic about his work has anything to fear from life. All the opportunities in the world are waiting to be grasped by people who are in love with what they're doing.*
>
> **Samuel Goldwyn**
> *Motion Picture Producer and Movie Industry Pioneer*

When you avoid hurtful gossip and bad office politics, you gain the trust of your team members and co-workers. Knowing when to speak and when to be silent is a valuable tool for any professional. For example, never correct another person in front of others, even if they are dead wrong. Remain silent. Ask to speak with him or her in private to point out the mistake. Take great pains to respect his or her dignity. More than likely, he or she will thank you for the correction and appreciate your discretion.

Assertiveness versus Aggressiveness

Assertiveness is the ability to express yourself and your rights without infringing on the rights of others. Being **assertive** means that you communicate honestly, openly, and directly in a way that clearly states your needs. People who are assertive gain the respect of those around them. Some people mistakenly believe that assertive means selfish. Selfishness is destructive and infringes on the rights of others. Assertiveness prevents people from taking advantage of you. You have the right to

- Change your mind.
- Ask for help or further information.
- Make mistakes.
- Assert your values, opinions, and beliefs.
- Express yourself and say "no" when you need to.
- Lead your life the way you see fit.
- Tell others how you wish to be treated.
- Develop or change your life.
- Have positive relationships where you feel comfortable and accepted.
- Like yourself even when you're not perfect.

People who lack assertiveness allow the needs, opinions, and judgments of others to become more important than their own. They react passively to situations. They experience anger, helplessness, fear, or frustration because of this behavior, which is dishonest and self-denying.

Assertive Actions

Assertive people are specific and clear about what they want. "I don't want you to hand-write the Nasby report. I want you to type it." "Would you please write a memo that informs all second-shift production workers about the flu vaccinations next week?" Assertiveness does not begin and end with conversation. Tone of voice, movements, posture, eye contact, and facial expressions also show assertiveness.

Assertive people communicate directly with the person who should receive the message. "Matt, your absenteeism has been excessive lately." Instead of: "Trudy, please remind Matt about our absenteeism policy."

Assertive people never suggest that someone is bad or wrong. They say, "I don't agree with you" rather than "You're wrong about that." Telling people that they are bad or wrong or should change because you think they should causes resentment and resistance.

Assertive people ask for feedback to correct any misconceptions. "I understand that you want me to get you the sales figures by next Friday, correct?"

Aggressive Actions

Being **aggressive** means that you express your rights at the expense of the rights of others. Aggressive people are manipulative and forceful. They show lack of respect

Figure 2.6 *You Decide*

Julian's Approach	Tyrone's Approach
Communicates clearly	Does not communicate well
Asks for feedback	Is unavailable for feedback or questions
Respects the opinions of others	Does not respect the opinions of others
Deals with problems directly	Avoids dealing with problems directly
Has the respect of his co-workers	Does not have the respect of his co-workers
Has the cooperation of his team members	Does not have the cooperation of his team members

Thinking Critically Manager Julian's approach will probably win his company the account. *What could Tyrone do to win back the respect of his team?*

for those around them. They command and demand without explanation: "Do it because I say so."

Aggressive people may achieve some limited success early in their career. However, in the long run, such people find their career stalling because they are unable to inspire cooperation in those who work for them. They command out of fear and not respect. They fail to earn the loyalty of those around them. Because aggressive people are poor communicators, the tasks they ask to have done may be done improperly and need to be repeated, which can be costly to the company.

Aggressiveness used to be prized in the workplace. Today, smart professionals recognize that teamwork and cooperation are much more effective than forced obedience. Today's diversified workforce demands that those in charge treat all who work for them and with them with respect and humanity.

Which Style Is Best?

Julian works for the ABC ad agency. Tyrone works for the XYZ ad agency. Both agencies are competing for the same high-dollar account with LMN, Inc., a breakfast food company. Winning this account can mean significant profits for both companies. Both Julian and Tyrone will lead their respective teams in the competition for the LMN account. They have both been given the information they need to begin work. Both are aware of the date they must present their ideas to the management at LMN, Inc. See Figure 2.6 to compare the two.

Julian's Approach   Julian meets with his team on the following morning to discuss the project. He has made a photocopy of all the information he received from the management team. He presents the information. He asks if everything is clear. He answers questions from the team. The team creates a schedule and team members volunteer for all the tasks that need to be done. They are ready to begin.

Early in the project, Brendon tells the team that his part of the project is more than he expected. Julian asks Brendon what he sees as a solution. Brendon tells the group that he talked the situation over with Sylvia. Sylvia is new and would like to have more responsibility. Julian asks Sylvia if she agrees. She does.

Sylvia has some concerns about Brendon, who is passing off too many of his duties to her. She feels overburdened. Julian says that he will speak with Brendon. He meets with Brendon that afternoon to set things straight.

The team meets to practice its presentation. Members of the group feel free to give their opinions and critique each person's part of the presentation. Gillian is concerned with some information in the marketing demographics portion of the presentation. Julian says, "I understand your concerns, but this source has been reliable for us in the past." The team members air all their concerns and work through the evening to fine-tune their presentation.

Julian and his team meet for dinner after their presentation. Everyone is very happy and comfortable with the work they did together. The LMN account means a lot to the company.

Tyrone's Approach   Tyrone meets with his team the next afternoon. That morning, he created a schedule and assigned everyone to a task. He has made one copy for the team to follow at the meeting. Tyrone is very busy that afternoon. At the meeting, he goes over the schedule and the assignments. He does not have time for questions. Team members are invited to ask Tyrone questions when they come up. They are not ready to begin. The team members are not sure what needs to be done; they are confused. Some team members are angry because they have been assigned to tasks that they do not perform well.

Early in the project, Tyrone meets with the entire team. They still have questions about what they should do. Some team members are complaining about their assignments. Tyrone has not been available to his team as promised to answer questions. They hope to have their questions and concerns addressed now, while they have him in the room. Tyrone becomes angry and says, "I want it done. I don't care how you do it, just get it done."

Tyrone's team meets without him because he is unavailable much of the time. They struggle with the project and are all worried for their jobs, because, although Tyrone leads the team, the entire team will be judged on the results. Josh tells the group that he went to Tyrone because of a problem he had getting information from the manager of the marketing department. Josh tells the team that Tyrone told him to "take care of his own problems."

Tyrone decides to attend the final meeting before the team must present its ideas to management. As the team presents its ideas for Tyrone, he becomes angry. "No! No, that's not what I wanted," he responds to all the ideas. "You better figure out something fast—before tomorrow! The LMN account means a lot to the company." He gets up and leaves.

The team is thoroughly frustrated now. They refuse to work on revisions at such a late date. The have all gone to dinner to discuss the fallout. They have no respect for Tyrone. They fear that they may lose their jobs, but they feel that this would be much better than to work with someone like Tyrone.

I'd Like to Thank . . .

Once you've been promoted, remember to thank all those who helped you get to where you are. Most likely, you were helped by people in both higher and lower positions than your own. If someone was particularly helpful, such as the manager who groomed you, consider sending a note and a small gift. Always treat everyone with the same respect, regardless of your position. The best thank-you, however, is to prove yourself to be a trained professional.

QUICK RECAP 2.5

MOVING UP: ACHIEVING GREATER INFLUENCE AND RESPECT

Now you should have a better idea of the benefits and importance of achieving greater influence and respect. Here is a quick summary:

• Building a relationship with your manager will set you apart from those just jockeying for promotion.
• Your opinion is valued when you build a reputation of respect and trust.
• Assertive people gain the respect of those around them.
• Aggressive people lose the respect of those around them.

CHECK YOURSELF

1. List five tips for how to act around and toward your manager.
2. Describe the differences between assertive and aggressive behavior.

Check your answers online at www.mhhe.com/pace. Pace ONLINE

BUSINESS VOCABULARY

assertive   expressing yourself and your rights without infringing on the rights of others
aggressive   expressing one's rights at the expense of the rights of others

Chapter Summary

2.1 Setting Benchmarks

Objective: Take the steps that will help you reach your goals.

In this section, you learned to create a career plan that includes measurable benchmarks. You read that successful professionals pay attention to all the aspects of their lives. You learned tips for working on your career goals within your current job.

2.2 Recognizing and Seizing Opportunities

Objective: Recognize and seize opportunities for advancement and promotion.

In this section, you learned the importance of establishing a relationship with your manager. You learned how to use job descriptions and job titles in your company. You discovered strategies to help you build your office network. You learned the importance of team building.

2.3 Broadening Knowledge and Skills

Objective: Learn the importance of continual learning.

In this section, you learned to take on more responsibility on your job, but beware of taking on too much, too soon. You examined the reasons why staying flexible helps protect you from being downsized. You looked at why reading, taking classes, and attending seminars and conferences makes you a valued employee. You learned that people who become complacent are too comfortable to take risks that lead to success.

2.4 Staying on the Right Track

Objective: Learn what to do to stay on track with your career goals.

In this section, you learned about the most common career pitfalls and how to avoid them. You learned why becoming involved in office intrigues and bad politics can hurt your reputation and credibility. On the other hand, you learned that good politics is an important and powerful tool. You discovered why and how to make a lateral move, how to deal gracefully with termination, when and how to move on gracefully, and what to do if you have to stay put.

2.5 Moving Up: Achieving Greater Influence and Respect

Objective: Learn what it takes to achieve greater influence.

In this section, you learned to build a relationship with your manager by communicating regularly, being well informed, and being a good professional. You discovered that to make your opinions matter, you need to build a reputation of respect and trust. You examined the difference between aggressive and assertive behavior styles and learned which one is more effective in today's business world.

Business Vocabulary

- 401(k) (p. 46)
- abstract services (p. 56)
- aggressive (p. 72)
- assertive (p. 72)
- benchmarks (p. 44)
- complacent (p. 56)
- cross-trained (p. 55)
- downsize (p. 55)
- job description (p. 51)
- lateral move (p. 64)
- multitasking (p. 62)
- nepotism (p. 67)
- prioritize (p. 62)
- promotion (p. 49)
- resignation (p. 65)
- telecommuting (p. 68)
- teleworking (p. 68)

Key Concept Review

1. Why is it important for you to include benchmarks in your career plan? (2.1)
2. Why do successful professionals pay attention to all aspects of their job? (2.1)
3. How does building a relationship with your manager pave the way to promotion? (2.2)
4. What is the importance of an in-house network? (2.2)
5. Why is flexibility important to today's professionals? (2.3)
6. How can the Internet assist you with continual learning? (2.3)
7. What are the dangers of limited identification? (2.4)
8. How can you improve your time management skills? (2.4)
9. Why is it important for you to know the goals of your manager? (2.5)
10. How can you be assertive and not aggressive? (2.5)

Online Project Pace ONLINE

Creating a Bibliography

A bibliography is a list of books that are used as references on a certain subject. When writing a research paper, you would include a bibliography of the books and sources you consulted to write the paper.

A great deal has been written on the subject of becoming more effective in work and in life. Search online at sites for your local public or college library, bookstores, and other resources and find books and magazine or journal articles related to this topic. Create a one-page bibliography of at least 10 sources. On a second page, write a phrase or sentence explaining why you chose each book and how you think it can help you learn to be more influential. Keep this bibliography as a research tool to help you learn more about this subject.

Step Up the Pace

CASE A   Turning a Temporary Job into a Career

You have been working as a temporary employee at a major corporation. You find out that you can ask your temp agency for a higher salary per hour if you are using specialized computer skills or software at your job. You know that the department you are assigned to needs someone with these skills and is thinking of bringing in another temp. You are already familiar with most of the software they are using but need a refresher course. You don't want to risk being replaced by someone else, but what can you do?

What to Do

1. Contact a temp agency, local job center, library, or community college in your area and find out what kinds of computer software training classes they offer at night. Make a chart comparing course content, cost, and the time commitment required.
2. Write a letter to your supervisor at the temp agency and the supervisor at your job telling them both about your plan to get additional training. Ask for a chance to tackle the higher-paying job.

CASE B   *Moving Up*

Your company is undergoing a major restructuring. You know that management will be combining some jobs and giving more responsibility to certain people. While most people are scared of what the restructuring will mean, you see it as an opportunity to move up. How do you go about it?

What to Do

1. Make a list of your accomplishments in your current job position, including such things as not taking any sick days, meeting deadlines, and extra work you've been doing outside of your regular job.
2. Write a letter to your manager describing your accomplishments and making a case for a promotion. Mention your interest in a new position and list what you have done recently to suggest you're ready for more responsibility.

Trouble-Free E-Mailing

E-mail is becoming more and more important in business communications. To make it as "user-friendly" as possible, use the following tips. Different systems will allow you to do different things, but you or your information technology department should be able to do all of the following:

- Set the margins to allow for 65 characters. This way the receiver won't see uneven lines.
- Send attachments in ASCII, Rich Text Format, or Text Only file. You don't always know what the receiver's word processing system is.
- Use spell-check before sending business mail.
- Add your full name, title, and phone number and/or extension to your signature. You also may want to add your fax number. Avoid personal mottos for business e-mail.
- Always type a subject in the Subject line.
- Avoid typing in all caps (all capital letters); this is like shouting.
- Reply to business e-mail within 24 hours of receiving it.
- If you will be away from the office for an extended period of time, set up an automatic reply to anyone who sends you e-mail during that time. Your IT person should be able to do this if you cannot.

Exercise: Retype the e-mail in Figure 2.7, correcting the mistakes.

Figure 2.7 *What Is Wrong with This E-Mail?*

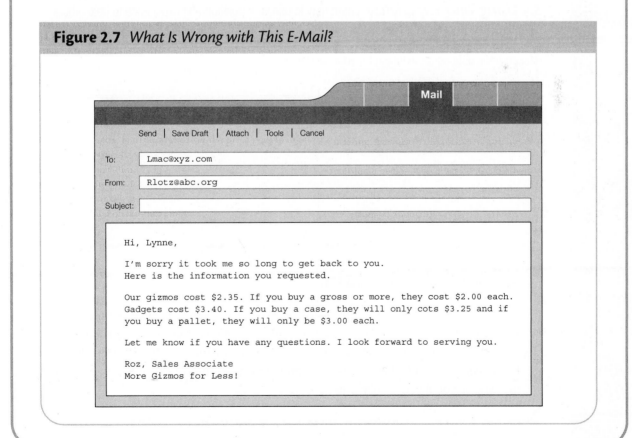

Maintain Your Career

What Will You Do?

3.1 Creating a Professional Reputation Learn what it takes to make a good name for yourself in today's business world.

3.2 Building and Maintaining a Professional Network Read about the importance of a professional network; learn how to stay in touch with your contacts.

3.3 Professional Pride: Taking and Giving Credit and Recognition Study the benefits of taking and giving credit in a team situation; discover why too much self-promotion is a bad thing.

3.4 Using Your Experience Learn how to use your position and experience to help others.

3.5 Working to Live versus Living to Work: Planning for the Long Run Research the options for planning for your retirement.

Why It's Important

You spent a good deal of time preparing for your career: going to school, getting to know yourself, researching companies, interviewing, making your career plan, creating a network. Now it's time to do the work necessary to maintain your career. It's also time to think about how and when you should end your career. Then again, maybe you won't retire. Maybe you'll begin a new career.

Chapter Objectives

After completing this chapter, you will be able to:

- Define your morals and values.

- Build and maintain your professional network.

- Explain why working in a team can be rewarding.

- Define what a mentor is and does.

- Extend your goals into the future.

Set the *Pace*

Your Long-Term Goals   Take time to think about your long-range goals. What do you see in your future? Remember that making a plan is the path to success. Write out your long-range career plan. Don't forget to include the benchmarks.

- Where do see yourself in 25, 30, 35, 40 years?
- When do you want to retire?
- Are you ready for a career change?

Activity   When you finish writing out your long-term career goals, break into groups of two. Share your career plan with the same partner you had when you created your 20-year plan. Offer honest suggestions and critique each other's plans. Talk about how you see yourself in retirement. What will you be doing?

Creating a Professional Reputation

In Section 2.4, you learned about good office politics and how you might begin to build a respectable reputation by practicing them. You also learned about the common career pitfalls that can damage your reputation. Here, you'll learn about the other things that make a good professional reputation.

Give Your Rep a Good Rap. Your reputation is the most important thing you have, and guarding it is your responsibility. You build a good professional reputation through your actions and deeds. You can't create a good reputation overnight; it takes awhile for people to see what kind of professional—and person—you truly are.

Reading and Study Tips

Inference
To make an inference means to come to a conclusion based on evidence or suggested ideas. In this section, there is a cartoon example based on two characters. At the end of the section, you are asked to make an inference about the two characters and what will happen to them. Write your conclusions on a separate sheet of paper.

values the beliefs that prompt one's behavior

morals standards upon which one judges what is good or bad, right or wrong

Making a Name for Yourself

Making a good name for yourself begins with your values and morals. **Values** are the beliefs that inspire your behavior. **Morals** are standards upon which you judge what is good or bad and right or wrong. How you act mirrors your values and morals. How you treat everyone you come in contact with says a lot about you as a professional. The skills and experience you have gained also contribute to your professional reputation. Fortunately or unfortunately, your value to your company is dependent on the name you make for yourself.

Who Are You?

In Chapter 1, you determined your strengths and weaknesses, your career and personal goals, your interests, your education, and your experiences. But do you know what is really important to you—what you value—and what you will do to get it. In other words, do you know your morals.

To know your values and morals will help with your career goals. Having this knowledge will help when there are tough decisions to make during the course of your career. The kind of decisions you make in your work life, as well as your personal life, shape your professional reputation. Take the time to look at your values and morals (see Figure 3.1).

Generally, the personal qualities most important to professionals include respect for self and others, trust, self-esteem, confidence, initiative, accountability, team spirit, customer focus, leadership skills, problem-solving skills, communication skills, and knowledge and experience.

Do Unto Others

When you practice the "golden rule" (do unto others as you would have done unto you), you begin to build a good reputation. Remember that this means *all* others, not just those who can help you. At worst, this means the production workers, maintenance staff, security staff, and administrative staff, as well as your superiors and co-workers. These people are an important part of any company. They have the power to influence.

Figure 3.1 *What Do You Value?*

_____ Have authority	_____ Power
_____ Chance for frequent promotion	_____ Money
_____ Be on the leading edge in my field	_____ Change and variety
_____ Help others	_____ Time for a personal life
_____ Help society	_____ Time with family and friends
_____ Meet challenges	_____ Fast-paced environment
_____ Public contact	_____ Risk taking
_____ Influence others	_____ Moral fulfillment
_____ Enjoy work tasks	_____ Recognition from peers, superiors,
_____ Enjoy work environment	and society
_____ Independence	_____ Clear expectations and procedures
_____ Working with others	_____ Chance to make an impact
_____ Personal growth and development	_____ Security
_____ Creativity	_____ Comfort
_____ Further learning	_____ Working alone
_____ Prestige	_____ Spirituality

Thinking Critically Read over the list of values. Rate their level of importance to you, using 4–not important, 3–somewhat important, 2–reasonably important, and 1– very important. Add to the list if you do not see something that is of value to you. *Choose the five values that are most important to you. What do your values say about your morals? How are they linked?*

Pace Points

Here Today; In Charge Tomorrow

If you always do the right thing and treat people the way you want to be treated, you don't have to worry about who's in charge. Remember, the intern or receptionist you treat poorly today may be your boss tomorrow. You never know when roles will be reversed or where people are headed. The intern you help out today will remember your help.

When you treat people with the dignity and respect they deserve, they become strong allies. They are willing to help you in a tight spot or lend a hand when you need it. They are willing to share important information that helps you get things done. They are willing to back you as you move ahead toward long-term success. The support of others is very important in today's business world. Remember that in order to maintain any respect you have earned, you have to be willing to give back to those who have given to you.

A Code of Ethics

Doing unto others in the professional sense is an important part of *ethics*. **Ethics** are the rules of conduct followed by a group or culture. Many professional associations create a **code of ethics,** or written rules of behavior for their members to follow. Doing anything unethical can cause you to be expelled from a company, group, or organization. See Figure 3.2 for a sample code of ethics.

Many companies create a code of ethics for their employees to follow. Employees are asked to read the codes and to sign their names as proof that they have understood

ethics the rules of conduct followed by a group or culture

code of ethics written rules of conduct for the members of a group or organization to follow

Figure 3.2 *The Fundamental Canon (Rules)*

The Fundamental Canon (Rules)

1. Engineers shall hold paramount the safety, health, and welfare of the public in the performance of their professional duties.

2. Engineers shall perform services only in the areas of their competence.

3. Engineers shall continue their professional development throughout their careers and shall provide opportunities for the professional and ethical development of those engineers under their supervision.

4. Engineers shall act in professional matters for each employer or client as faithful agents or trustees, and shall avoid conflicts of interest or the appearance of conflicts of interest.

5. Engineers shall build their professional reputation on the merit of their services and shall not compete unfairly with others.

6. Engineers shall associate only with reputable persons or organizations.

7. Engineers shall issue public statements only in an objective and truthful manner.

8. Engineers shall consider environmental impact in the performance of their professional duties.

Thinking Critically These are the fundamental canons of the code of ethics of the American Society of Mechanical Engineers (ASME). *Could the code of ethics for mechanical engineers be followed by other organizations?*

> **❝** *The education of a man is never completed until he dies.* **❞**
>
> **Robert E. Lee**
> *Confederate General during the Civil War*

and will follow the code. The code of ethics protects the company from legal problems created by unethical behavior of its employees. A company's code of ethics will spell out where it stands on issues such as conflicts of interest, second jobs, discriminatory actions, trade secrets, how to use company property, and political activities.

Skills, Credentials, and Experience

The skills, credentials, and experience you bring to the workplace are all part of your reputation. Skills that promote a good professional reputation include trust building, leadership, team spirit, problem solving, and good communication. These are the skills you use everyday.

credentials education and professional knowledge gained, such as degrees and certificates

Your **credentials** include education and professional knowledge—degrees and certificates. Do you have the educational background and professional knowledge that fits your position? When you make a decision or take a risk, do you have the background education and professional knowledge to make an informed decision or take a calculated risk?

Your experience comes from past jobs. What did you do on your last job? Were you able to complete your projects on time and under budget? Does your past experience help with your current job? What did you learn from the past? What did you learn from your mistakes? What did you learn from your success?

The Value of a Good Reputation

Michiko and Keilani are both sales associates. Both are new employees who work for separate telecommunications companies. See Figure 3.3.

Figure 3.3 *You Be the Judge*

Michiko's Approach	Keilani's Approach
Motivated by career choice	Motivated by money
Eager to learn about the company, sales techniques, and product	Eager to begin making commissions and single-handedly making her team number one
Has the admiration, respect, and trust of her team	Has her team discussing her transfer to another department
Does not take advantage of her company	Tries to take advantage of her company
Tries to make practical deals that will work for everyone	Makes any promises to get the sale
An asset to the team and company	A short-term asset but a future problem for the team and company

Thinking Critically Now, Keilani enjoys early financial success, but can Keilani look for greater success in the future? *Which woman is most likely to receive the support of others in reaching her career goals?*

Michiko's Approach Michiko is the newest member of the team that targets East Coast sales. She is eager to learn about the company, the selling techniques it uses, and the product she will be selling: phone and networking systems to large companies. The team meets to bring her up to speed on how they work. This team has built a reputation of being the company's top seller and is number one when it comes to repeat sales. Michiko appreciates the support her team gives her.

After she completes training, Michiko meets with her first customer over lunch. Mr. Brunswick wants a new system set up in his offices in half the usual time at half the price. Michiko doesn't want to make any promises her installers can't keep. Michiko checks with her office and offers him a more realistic deal. Disappointed, Mr. Brunswick says that he'll get back with her. She pays for lunch and says that she looks forward to doing business with him.

Michiko enjoys the perks of her job, including an expense account and all the latest cell technology. Remembering that it was provided mainly so she could do her job better, she does try to use it responsibly. She uses the company credit card only for company business. Although they would be useful to keep, Michiko saves freebies with the company logo for customers only.

Michiko is getting a slow start for the year, but her team is encouraging. Michiko has gained their admiration, respect, and trust. Though her numbers for repeat sales are greater than her sales volume, repeat sales say good things about the team and the company. The rest of the team has decided that they will move Michiko from established customers to new customers by next year. She has proved to be a valued member to the team and to the company.

Keilani's Approach Keilani's team is number two in East Coast sales but is closing in on the number one team at EFG Telecommunications. She meets with the team. They plan their strategy for improving sales and taking over the number one

Ten Ways You Can Build Your Professional Reputation

• **Do your best work.** Try to always do your best. You never know who will see it.

• **Keep your promises.** Don't make promises unless you *know* you can deliver.

• **Meet your deadlines.** Do what you can and get help if needed. If you absolutely cannot meet the deadline, let people know right away.

• **Take responsibility and share credit.** Admit your mistakes. Acknowledge the people who helped you. Doing both will actually make you look good!

• **Go the extra mile.** If adding something will actually be helpful, do it. Find the figures from last year's sales, retype your report, or cc your boss on a memo. A little extra work could pay off big time in the long run.

• **Be ready to help your colleagues as well as your clients.** Good rapport around the office can be crucial to your career.

• **Make a good impression with everyone you meet.** Receptionists, interns, janitors, and factory workers also can be valuable allies—don't miss your chance.

• **Take on challenges and try new things.** You never know what new skills you may develop or hidden talents you may find!

• **Be an optimist and focus on the positive.** It may be easier to be negative, but staying positive will be more helpful to you and those around you.

• **Act with integrity and style in everything you do.** One compromise leads to more. Don't compromise your values—or yourself.

spot. Keilani is eager to begin selling—she doesn't care what—and making commissions. She feels that planning and teamwork are wasting her time. "How difficult can it be to sell phones?" she thinks.

Keilani is excited about her first sales call with a new customer. She is meeting Mr. Brunswick, a customer of the competition. Keilani is already dreaming of her first commission and single-handedly making her team number one. Again, Mr. Brunswick asks for installation of a phone network in half the time at half price. Keilani smiles and says, "I look forward to doing business with you, Mr. Brunswick." Keilani goes back to her team to brag that she stole a customer from the competitor, but she does not give the details about the deal.

Keilani looks for any excuse to use the expense account and to keep the freebies she's supposed to be giving to clients. She'll mention her work when out with friends, then call it "doing business" in order to use her company credit card. Also, she enjoys having the latest technology. When anything new comes out, Keilani demands to be the first to try it.

Although Keilani's installers worked overtime, they couldn't install the new system for Mr. Brunswick's company as fast as she promised. Mr. Brunswick vowed never to use HIJ Telecommunications again. Accounting and upper management are also displeased with the discount Keilani gave. Keilani is interested only in new sales and commissions.

Keilani's team is number one in East Coast sales volume this year. Her team members are happy to be number one but are concerned about their drop in repeat sales. Her team members do not admire, trust, or respect her actions. They are worried about the team's reputation. Several members want her to be transferred to another department because she lacks understanding of the basic principles of business and sales.

Your Value to the Company

Your value to your company is a combination of your skills, your credentials, and your experience. Does your presence add value to the company? People with a good professional reputation are good for any company. The reputation of a company relies on the people who work for it. A good reputation sells better than any high-priced advertising. The other values you can bring to your job include accountability, a customer-focused attitude, problem-solving skills, and initiative, as well as leadership, team spirit, trust building, self-esteem, and confidence.

Pace Points

Referrals

Building a good professional reputation is a smart career move. If people know that you do good work and are ethical, they will have no problem referring you to friends or colleagues for jobs. If the person they refer turns out to be terrible, it makes them look bad as well, so they will only give opportunities to people whose reputation they can trust.

QUICK RECAP 3.1

CREATING A PROFESSIONAL REPUTATION

Now you should have a better idea of the benefits and importance of creating a professional reputation. Here is a quick summary:

- A good professional reputation is created through your actions and deeds.
- Making a good name for yourself begins with your values and morals.
- The kind of decisions you make in your work and personal life shapes your professional reputation.
- Practice the golden rule: begin to build your good reputation.
- Your value to any company comes from a combination of how you treat others, your skills, your credentials, and your experience.

CHECK YOURSELF

1. What personal qualities are most important to any professional?
2. Explain why companies have a code of ethics.

Check your answers online at www.mhhe.com/pace. Pace ONLINE

BUSINESS VOCABULARY

values   the beliefs that prompt one's behavior
morals   standards upon which one judges what is good or bad, right or wrong
ethics   the rules of conduct followed by a group or culture
code of ethics   written rules of conduct for the members of a group or organization to follow
credentials   education and professional knowledge gained, such as degrees and certificates

In Chapters 1 and 2, you learned about the importance of networking. You learned how to build a network that contains acquaintances and people from your in-house office life. Here, you will learn about the importance of building and maintaining a professional network.

What Is a Professional Network?   A professional network consists of people with whom you do business outside of your office. It works in the same manner as your in-house network. You build a list of people you can help and who can help you with information and support. Your professional network can offer valuable information about new positions or openings, about shifts in your career field, or about changes that may affect your current position.

The Professional Network

Your professional network should contain people who have the same or similar morals and values. The reputations of the people in your network are a reflection of your reputation. Since you took the time to look at your own morals and values, you are in a better position to choose reputable, valuable network contacts. Here are some tips to help build your professional network:

- Join professional groups, associations, and organizations in your career field. Introduce yourself, pass out your business card, exchange information, volunteer for committee work.
- Attend seminars and conferences. Introduce yourself to others, pass out your business card, exchange information, spend your lunch break with others attending the same conference, volunteer to be a speaker.
- If you are taking classes to further your education, join a study group, join some campus activities, build a relationship with your instructor, volunteer to tutor another student.
- In business, show your professionalism everyday, build a good reputation, exchange information, volunteer for public service work, respect your network.
- Refer to the Internet networking strategies in Chapter 1.

Keeping in Touch with Your Professional Acquaintances

The people in your professional network can be other businesspeople with whom you have exchanged business cards. They can be people you met at seminars and conferences. They can be classmates and instructors you met while furthering your education. They can be fellow members of a professional association or group.

You learned in earlier chapters that building a network helps when you remember that the relationship is one of give and take. Keeping in touch with those network contacts is very important.

Figure 3.4 Your Professional Networking Journal

Name: Julia Wozniack (nickname JJ)

Telephone: Work 606-555-4562   **Home** 606-555-1204

Fax: 606-555-4560   **E-mail:** jjwo@trace.com   **Web site:** www.trace.com

Job Title: General Sales Manager

Company: Trace Farm Implements

Address: 200 Tractor Place, Suite 203, Lexington, KY

Birthday: August 23, 1960 (Ashland, KY)

Family: Married (second husband, Thomas [12/22/58], independent construction contractor), two children (Candice, 15 [4/6/90], and Cameron, 20 [6/19/85]), three stepchildren (Grayson, 6 [11/8/99], Jennifer, 8 [7/23/97], and Keith, 16 [6/1/89]) share custody with mother. Cameron in school at Ohio State University, majoring in ag science. #3 runner on the OSU cross country team

Education: BS in Agri-business from Morehead State University and The Ohio State University Fisher College of Business. MBA, recently obtained

Affiliations: The Kentucky Antique Farm Machinery Association member for 14 years. Member of the National Agri-Business Association, 5 years

Interests and Accomplishments: Collects and restores John Deere tractors, farms 100 acres on the family farm, follows OSU cross country and football

Thinking Critically Updating your contact information from time to time is good business. *How would you go about updating your contact information without directly asking?*

A Network Journal The best way of keeping track of important information about your network contacts is to keep a networking journal like the one you used in Chapter 1. As you can see in Figure 3.4, the journal you keep for your professional contacts can contain even more detail.

Computer "Journals" If you'd rather keep your network information electronically, you can use a hand-held PDA (*p*ersonal *d*ata *a*ssistant, such as a Palm Pilot), which keeps track of names and telephone numbers. If you prefer using your computer, there are several methods available. Business contact software works like a **database system,** which stores all like information in the same place, called a *field*. But business contact software does much more than the standard database. Some can send e-mail reminders to help you make contact periodically. Some can help you search for and exchange information on the Internet. Others can help you follow up on a sales call with an e-mail, letter, or fax in the time period you suggest.

database system a computer program that stores all like information in the same place

The Dangers of Burning Bridges, Backstabbing, and Bad-Mouthing

The professional who wants to maintain his or her good reputation does not badmouth co-workers, teammates, previous employers, managers, past and current company, customers or vendors, network contacts, or competitors. Even if you feel you have a trusted friend at the office with whom you can share your thoughts on co-workers or contacts, that individual might feel that he or she has other trusted friends to whom he or she can tell, and so forth. Before long, your bad-mouthing has been added to, changed, and spread throughout the office. Your reputation has been damaged. Your in-house network is worthless.

Backstabbing your co-workers, teammates, manager, or network contacts can do damage to your reputation and to your career. The respect and trust others felt for you is lost. You are kept out of the communication loop. You are looked on as a person to be either avoided or watched with caution. You are passed up for promotion because of your actions. It's very difficult, if not impossible, to repair the damage done by hurtful words and actions.

Burning bridges happens when you leave one company, one department, one team, or one position for another in an unprofessional manner. An unprofessional exit can damage any good you have done to your network, your reputation, and your chances for career advancement. The successful professional builds bridges instead of burning them.

> **"** *There are two things people want more than sex and money—recognition and praise.* **"**
>
> *Mary Kay Ash*
> *Founder of Mary Kay Cosmetics*

Building Bridges

In Chapter 2, you learned how to gracefully leave one company for another. These rules also apply when making a lateral move to another department, team, or position within the same company. Additionally, you can offer to train your replacement and act as a resource for him or her. Leave correctly filled-in samples of forms or any other aids needed to do the job. Leave behind a clean, organized workspace.

During your last week, talk one-on-one with each current co-worker. Let each co-worker know what you learned from him or her, what strengths or skills he or she has that you admire, or even what contribution you think he or she will make in the future. Keep your bonds strong with the department and the people you are leaving. You never know when you may need their goodwill. When you build bridges, you strengthen your network and your professional reputation. Both greatly increase your chances for career success.

The Importance of Loyalty and Personal Commitment

Anyone who has played on a sports team knows the importance of loyalty and personal commitment. When all the players are working toward the same goal, the team has a much better chance of winning the championship.

Companies work the same way. They set goals to help them be successful in the marketplace. They hire people to help them meet these goals. To help their employees understand these goals, they write a **mission statement** that defines their business, its purpose, and its values, as in the one in Figure 3.5.

mission statement a written statement of a company's purpose, business, and values

Purpose   The *purpose* of the National Weather Service is to "provide weather, hydrologic, and climate forecasts and warnings for the United States, its territories, adjacent waters and ocean areas."

Business   The NWS's *business* provides "NWS data and products [that] form a national information database and infrastructure which can be used by other governmental agencies, the private sector, the public, and the global community."

Values   The NWS's *values* cover "the protection of life and property and the enhancement of the national economy."

Burning Bridges

Your Challenge

For the past two years, you have worked for a manager you don't like. You have no respect for how she does business, treats employees, and does her job. You have stuck it out this long to get enough experience to move to a better position. You have finally found the job you want and it's your last day at work. You are on your way out the door for good and you have one more chance to say your piece to your manager. What do you do?

The Possibilities

A. Let her have it. Tell her exactly what you think of her and what she can do with her job. You don't ever have to go back, so who cares?

B. Skip it. Leave without saying goodbye. You are done with her now and have no more reason to talk to her.

C. Drop by her office and say goodbye. Be courteous without being phony and say that you've learned a lot and have appreciated the experience. Wish her luck and leave as a professional.

D. Lay it on thick. Give her a big hug and tell her how much you'll miss her, and how you'll have to keep in touch because you've learned so much working for her. Stroke her ego so she'll regret not being nicer to you when you worked there.

Your Solution

Choose the solution that you think will be most effective and write a few sentences explaining your opinion. Then check your answer with the answer on our Web site: **www.mhhe.com/pace.**

Pace ONLINE

Figure 3.5 *Mission Statement of the National Weather Service*

"The National Weather Service (NWS) provides weather, hydrologic, and climate forecasts and warnings for the United States, its territories, adjacent waters and ocean areas, for the protection of life and property and the enhancement of the national economy. NWS data and products form a national information database and infrastructure which can be used by other governmental agencies, the private sector, the public, and the global community."

Thinking Critically The mission statement gives a broad definition of its industry and company goals. *What would the mission statement for a company in your career field look like?*

Go Forth and Build

Successful professionals are loyal and personally committed to their work. They do their best every time. They are loyal and personally committed to their co-workers, their teammates, and their company. They are part of the team that helps their company be successful. When the company wins, everyone wins.

BUILDING AND MAINTAINING
A PROFESSIONAL NETWORK

Now you should have a better idea of the benefits and importance of building and maintaining a professional network. Here is a quick summary:

- Your professional network should contain people who have the same or similar morals and values.
- Practicing bad politics, such as backstabbing and bad-mouthing, can hurt your chances for promotion.
- Companies hire people who are loyal and committed to helping them reach their goals so they can be successful in the marketplace.

CHECK YOURSELF

1. What are potential results of backstabbing your co-workers?
2. Name the three things that make up a mission statement.

Check your answers online at www.mhhe.com/pace.

BUSINESS VOCABULARY

database system   a computer program that stores all like information in the same place
mission statement   a written statement of a company's purpose, business, and values

In today's fast-pace world of business, successful professionals recognize the importance of visibility. **Visibility** involves doing good work and letting others know about it—putting your name and accomplishments out there for all to see. In an ideal world, every boss would recognize and reward good work without being asked. Since that doesn't always happen, however, you need to make sure your manager knows about your good work.

Shine On!   Visibility in the workplace also involves working well and sharing credit with others, especially when you work as part of a team. It's part of the reputation you build, part of the network you build, part of everything that says you are a professional.

Self-Promotion Do's and Don'ts

Successful professionals recognize that success takes more than doing your best at your job. It takes more than meeting your deadlines. It takes more than coming in under budget. You had to "sell" yourself to get the job. Now that you have it, you still have to sell yourself to keep moving toward your goals.

Self-promotion must be handled carefully. If you tell everyone you see about your good work all the time, you come across as a braggart. But if you remain quiet about your accomplishments, you may not get that promotion. People who make themselves visible rise quicker than quiet ones with superior abilities.

Find ways to insert your accomplishments easily into conversation (see Chapter 2, p. 60, "Pitfalls You Already Know"). Write a report for your manager at the end of a project. If you are working on a project that may be of public interest, volunteer to handle getting publicity. Don't forget to include, or at least give credit to, everyone involved with the project.

Working as Part of a Team

In Chapter 2, you learned about team building and what it takes to be a valuable team member. You learned that a few people working toward a common goal can accomplish more than many people working alone. Businesses find that people who work in teams can produce more in a more efficient manner.

Working in a team has many advantages for the team's members. **Collaboration,** or working together, takes advantage of the strengths of every team member. **Motivation,** or the will to act, comes from enjoying the work and knowing that others depend on you to do your part. When collaboration is good and motivation is high, trust is built into the team. Selfishness and competition have no place on a successful team.

Often, though, teams are unable to find ways to work together. There may be some weak members on the team. If you find yourself in such a team, rise above and take the other members with you. They may, by your example, come around to the "team way of thinking."

visibility   involves doing good work and letting others know about it

Reading and Study Tips

Characteristics
Characteristics are physical, emotional, and personality traits of a character. A person's characteristics can help you determine what kind of values he or she has. For example, a greedy person might be selfish or a kind person might be generous. Similarly, a person's behavior can help you determine his or her characteristics. Look at the example using characters in this section. Identify characteristics of each person based on his or her behavior in the example.

❝ *It ain't bragging if you can do it.* ❞

Jay "Dizzy" Dean
Former Professional Baseball Player

collaboration   working together

motivation   the will to act

Figure 3.6 *You Be the Judge*

Stefan's Approach	Greg's Approach
Has had previous successes	Has had previous successes
Has built and maintains a good professional reputation	Has a questionable reputation in spite of his successes
Has a good working relationship with the team	Attends to team business only when upper management is present
Gives credit to all team members	Takes the credit for himself
Keeps open the line of communication with all members	Hides important details from the team

Thinking Critically Obviously, Stefan will be the one to enjoy long-term success. *What kind of damage has Greg done to his career and reputation? How would the actions of the team promote its members' careers and reputations?*

Dr. Joe Pace
TEAMWORK

"Teamwork is the ability to work together toward a common vision. The ability to direct individual accomplishments toward organizational objectives. It is the fuel that allows common people to attain uncommon results."

Taking Credit as a Team

Use the word "we" instead of "I" when talking about the team and its accomplishments. Don't forget to "sell" your entire team and give credit to all its members. When a member of the team has the opportunity to rise, he or she will remember whether or not you took all the credit for yourself. Your willingness to share credit reflects on your reputation and your professionalism.

Taking Credit

Stefan and Greg work together on the same city planning team. Both bring to the team a history of past successes. The team members know each other but have never worked together on the same team. The team votes to make Stefan and Greg co-leaders of the team. Their current project is to come up with a plan to revitalize a depressed area of the city. This project, if successful, will be a boost to all team members. See Figure 3.6.

Stefan's Approach   The project begins with the team taking a tour of the site to be included in the plan. Everyone is present except Greg. Stefan asks the others if anyone knows where Greg is. Ellie tells the group, "Greg said something about an important lunch appointment; he didn't say with whom." Stefan thanks Ellie and does not comment on Greg's absence. The team continues the tour. Stefan decides that he will bring Greg up to speed in the afternoon.

Stefan stops by Greg's office in the afternoon. He does not ask Greg where he was. He brings Greg up to speed on the project's progress so far. Greg volunteers to handle all the public relations (PR) for the project. It's the first thing Greg has offered to do, so Stefan agrees.

Greg rarely shows up for team meetings. The team keeps him informed of meeting times and the progress of the project. Greg only comes to meetings when upper

Tips From a Mentor

Ten Ways to Promote Yourself and Your Team without Being a Show-Off

- *Send periodic updates to your network* by e-mail asking what they are working on and sharing your news and projects with them. They will pass the word on.

- *Update your profile* on your campus or alumni Web site or in professional organizations adding your most recent job assignments or accomplishments in a down-to-earth way.

- *Tell your personal network*—mom, dad, family, hairdresser, or friends—who are very proud of you what you have been doing. They will promote you shamelessly and no one will hold it against you if your mom thinks you are great.

- *Pass praise along.* If a customer or client tells you they have had a great experience with you and writes to thank you, forward the message to your supervisor. Just say you wanted to show them the nice letter that someone wrote you (that just happens to sing your praises).

- *Build your reference file.* Ask for letters of recommendation when you leave a job or department. Choose a boss or employer who likes your work to use as your reference on job applications. Let them promote you to potential employers.

- *Don't be shy.* In a job interview, tell prospective employers why you are right for a job, what your accomplishments have been, and how you can help their company.

- *Be sincere.* If you volunteer, have hobbies, do charitable work, or have a part of your life that is meaningful to you, share it with your employers. Let them know that there are things that you care deeply about and that you are proud of all the work you do.

- *Be humble.* Sometimes being humble or not boasting about your own accomplishments is the best way to make them visible. Promote your team and the people who help you in your efforts. That is the mark of a true leader and a true professional.

- *Volunteer to speak* about your work, company, or projects at clubs, professional associations, or volunteer associations. Mentor students and new employees and make a good impression. Good work from people you trained is a good reflection of your ability.

- *Be memorable.* Look your best, feel your best, smile, enjoy your life and work, and make people feel good when they meet you. This makes you stick out in a crowd.

---

management will be present. Then, he shares the stage with Stefan. Stefan makes certain he mentions the names of all the team members and their role in the project.

Greg's Approach   At the beginning of the project, Greg makes a lunch engagement with the local newspaper editor. Greg does not tell his team about the interview. The editor asks Greg to meet with a reporter at the site and poses for a picture without his team. He cannot remember the names of everyone on the team, so he calls them "the planning team." He doesn't get all the details correct, but at least the public will know about the project.

After the newspaper article appears, the mayor calls Stefan's boss with concerns. Greg's team is hurt that he went behind their backs. Stefan is even more upset that he has to spend extra time soothing the mayor and diplomatically explaining the problem to upper management. Stefan is still polite with Greg and still keeps him updated—when it is convenient for him. Greg has lost allies in the company.

The project has been completed successfully. Unfortunately, it did not meet the deadline because of extra red tape with the mayor's office. Because of the difficulties, it will not be as much of a boost as it could have been for them. The team has an unofficial celebration because they do not want to invite Greg.

Using Your Successes to Build Your Professional Profile

You are doing well at your first job. You have built and maintained a strong professional and in-house network. You have built a good professional reputation. Now you are ready for greater challenges. You may need to think about moving on to reach your career goals.

Now you have real work experience and added skills to dress up your résumé. Your references are strong because of your reputation for good work. You have added your successes to your career portfolio. The people in your network have been notified that you are on the market. You have sent each contact a copy of your updated résumé. Now, it's time to put that network to work.

Because you have taken the time to plan and consciously create your professional profile, your path to your career goals is made much easier. Finding new, rewarding work and opportunities is a breeze. People will know who you are and what you have done and can guess what you might do in the future—because you have "shown" them.

QUICK RECAP 3.3

PROFESSIONAL PRIDE: TAKING AND GIVING CREDIT AND RECOGNITION

Now you should have a better idea of the benefits and importance of developing professional pride. Here is a quick summary:
• Successful professionals recognize the importance of self-promotion.
• People who work successfully in teams can produce more in a more efficient manner.
• Your positive professional profile makes reaching your career goals much easier.

CHECK YOURSELF

1. Which word should you use when talking about the team and its accomplishments?
2. Name two things that help build your professional profile.

Check your answers online at **www.mhhe.com/pace.**

BUSINESS VOCABULARY

collaboration   working together
motivation   the will to act
visibility   involves doing good work and letting others know about it

Using Your Experience

You are rising in the ranks. You're reaching your benchmarks. You're attaining your goals. You have helped many people along the way. Many people have helped you. Your first manager took you under her wing and helped guide your career. Today, she is a senior vice president and you are not far behind. Now it's time for you to help others, for you to give informational interviews, for you to give references, for you to help those just beginning their careers.

Helping Out. There are several ways for you to help others. You can become a mentor to a younger person at work. You can tutor children or college students. You can be a good manager. You can help in your community with service or charity work. When you find ways to help others, you promote your professionalism. You cement the word "good" to your reputation.

Becoming a Mentor

A **mentor** is a person who gives advice to others and helps them learn and grow to their fullest potential. Mentors are knowledgeable about their subject, practice patience, and have excellent communication skills. They help the people they mentor with "ins and outs" of the company and its politics. Mentoring is a relationship based on mutual respect and trust. It means that you are a role model. You set a good example by listening, leading, discussing issues, and challenging others to be and do their best. You help others because you were helped.

Mentors have a responsibility to those who come to them for help. Because of the close relationship developed, the mentor may find him- or herself dealing with the emotional issues of the mentoree. The duties of a mentor do not include counseling. You put yourself and your company at risk when you become involved in a mentoree's emotional problems. Refer the mentoree to a professional counselor or to your human resources department. When you understand the boundaries of mentoring, you are better able to help others.

Mentors as Trainers

Many companies today have their own mentoring programs. Because budgets have been slashed to cut costs, training teams have been eliminated. Mentoring programs help reduce employee training costs. They also assist in giving the company periodic information about the progress of the mentoree. But this is not always the best way to pair mentors and mentorees. Some people just don't want to be mentored. This can lead to an unproductive situation. Speak with your manager as soon as possible if it looks as if your mentoring partnership isn't going to work. There is no time to waste in finding the right person to mentor.

You can find other opportunities to mentor in professional organizations, such as the ones to which you belong. Your network also can assist with finding mentoring opportunities. It won't be too difficult to find eager young people who would welcome your guidance and support.

> ### Reading and Study Tips
>
> *Reference*
> This section includes references to different organizations. A reference is a source of more information about the topic referred to. On a separate sheet of paper, make a list of other sources of information, excluding Web sites, that can be used as references on this topic.

mentor a person who gives advice to others and helps them learn and grow to their fullest potential

Being a Mentor

Your Problem

You have just volunteered to be a mentor to a new employee at your company. Your new mentoree is more interested in schmoozing with influential people than in finding out the best way to work for the company. He is very nice, and he seems to know the business—at least, as well as a new person should. Still, he doesn't seem to want to spend any time listening to what you have to say unless you're introducing him to someone in upper management. What do you do?

The Possibilities

A. Complain to his boss. Explain that your mentor has given you no attention and doesn't respect you at all. Tell his boss to consider firing him.

B. Ignore the situation. Decide to leave him to his schmoozing and hope he figures out what he needs to know on his own. Perhaps he'll make enough of a fool of himself that he'll decide he wants to be mentored after all.

C. Find a new mentoree. Take the initiative to find someone you do like who is interested in being mentored and work with that person.

D. Ask your mentoree for a regular weekly meeting time when you can catch up and discuss his training. Help him to set tasks for himself that will help him get the attention he wants. If he is still not interested, discuss the problem with the program supervisor.

Your Solution

Choose the solution that you think will be most effective and write a few sentences explaining your opinion. Then check your answer with the answer on our Web site: **www.mhhe.com/pace.**

Using Your Position to Help, Not Harm

When you move up in rank or in position, you gain new and greater power. You can use this power to help or to harm. Many people in managerial positions tend to misuse their power. To avoid using your power to harm, steer clear of unethical behavior and become involved in community service or charity work.

The Good Boss

The good boss leads by example. He or she keeps his or her emotions under control. He or she takes responsibility for the work and actions of those he or she manages. Being a good boss is much like being a mentor. Many times you actually become the mentor of your employees. When your employees conduct themselves with professionalism, such behavior is a direct reflection on you. Their good work is your good work.

Here are some other qualities that will help make you the good boss:

- Do everything you can to help your employees be able to do good work.
- Give them the proper tools and resources to do the job.
- Set goals for the department and communicate them to your employees.
- Help your employees set individual goals.
- Communicate often.
- Coach them to solve their own problems.
- Model taking responsibility; do not tolerate blaming others.

- Respond to problems positively instead of reacting to them emotionally.
- Be honest.
- Have a positive and grateful attitude.
- Have an open mind; there is no one right way.
- Respect the differences among your employees.
- Listen and speak without judgment.
- Steer clear of assumption; ask questions to avoid misconceptions and misunderstandings.
- Be a good role model; model your professionalism.

Avoid Unethical Behavior

They say that power corrupts. Unethical behavior can harm the reputation and profitability of your company. It also can harm your reputation and your chances for further advancement. Furthermore, it sends the wrong message to the people who look up to you.

Community Service and Charity Work

Community service and charity work are rewarding on their own. It's rewarding to give our time, money, and energy to making someone's life better. We are doubly rewarded for our good works because unselfish service and giving are connected to the "good" in good reputation. Because you hold a high position in your company and your community and have made a good name for yourself, your name can lend strength to a cause, can bring in more dollars and support. So, both you and your charity will benefit.

School Partnerships

School partnerships and mentoring programs for school-age children and college students are other ways of giving. In a school partnership, a business adopts a school. The business allows release time for volunteering employees, usually an hour a week, to help out at the school. They may read to kids, give talks about their job, or help with tutoring. The partnership gives the business a good name. The school benefits from the volunteers and usually from the generosity of the business. A business may help provide computers or other necessary tools and materials to the partner school.

Mentoring Programs

The Internet has many mentoring sites, such as the National Mentoring Partnership and the National Mentoring Center. You can help troubled or disabled children meet the challenges of life and give them the benefit of your experience and time. Many college and alumni associations have mentoring programs that allow you to be partnered with a college student in your career field. You can help open doors for a young graduate much the same way someone else did for you.

Staying Diverse and Applying What You've Learned

The key to keeping any career from getting stale is to stay diverse and continue learning. If you have actually achieved all the goals you set out to achieve, you should make a whole new set of goals and go after them. Maybe it involves starting your own business or beginning a new career.

> *Always remember that no matter how successful you are or what you achieve, there are others who are going through difficult times and dealing with serious problems in their lives. Be a quiet role model.*
>
> *Nicholas Pratt*
> *Author*

Many people change careers after they have reached all of their current goals. They choose to follow a new path—one that is less about making money and more about enjoyment. They set new goals. Many people also choose to start their own businesses. These people are called **entrepreneurs.** They have ideas about ways to do things better.

For example, while Chandra was researching her master's degree thesis on computer security systems, she accidentally came across information about graphic design programs. Chandra had always been the creative type. She enjoyed her high school and undergrad art classes. This information stuck with her over the years. When she found herself growing bored with her position as the head of her company's research and development department, she went back to school to study graphic design. Today, she does freelance graphic design from her home. She is able to spend more time with her family and aging mother, do what she loves, and earn a comfortable living.

QUICK RECAP 3.4

USING YOUR EXPERIENCE

Now you should have a better idea of the benefits and importance of using your experience. Here is a quick summary:

- A mentor is a role model for others.
- The good boss leads by example.
- Your unethical behavior can harm the reputation and profitability of your company.
- Many people change careers after they have reached all of their goals.

CHECK YOURSELF

1. Name three ways to become a mentor.
2. Name three qualities that make a good boss.

Check your answers online at **www.mhhe.com/pace.** *Pace* ONLINE

BUSINESS VOCABULARY

entrepreneurs   people who start their own businesses
mentor   a person who gives advice to others and helps them learn and grow to their fullest potential

Working to Live versus Living to Work: Planning for the Long Run

You spent time early in your career making your career plan. This plan helped you make informed decisions about your career. You became successful by achieving your goals. A successful retirement also must be planned. Where will you get income, for example? What new expenses will you have?

Start saving now. It is never too early to begin thinking about and saving for retirement. In fact, the earlier you begin, the more you will earn. Here, you will learn about some options to help you meet your long-term goals.

Considering Retirement Savings Plans, Health Care, Educational Savings

Along with your salary, most, if not all, companies provide benefits to their full-time employees. Benefit packages usually include either retirement savings plans or pension plans, and health care. Companies do not provide for educational or college savings plans.

Retirement

Most companies help provide for the retirement of their employees. Long past are the days when Americans could retire solely on Social Security. In fact, there is much doubt about the future of the Social Security system. Company pension funds have received a lot of bad press lately. They look more and more unreliable as a means of retirement funding. Today's professionals shouldn't depend solely on such shaky systems for their retirement.

Planning for your retirement is just as important as planning for your career. In Chapter 1, you got to know yourself and your practical needs. You can apply this knowledge to planning for your retirement. These are some questions you should ask yourself:

- When do I want to retire?
- How long do I have until I retire?
- What are my goals?
- How much will I need?
- How much should I save currently to meet my goals and needs?
- What kind of investor am I? Am I aggressive or conservative? Do I prefer high or low risk?

Knowing the answer to these questions will help you make better decisions. If you are an aggressive investor and don't mind high risk, you'll gamble on the stock market. If you are conservative and want low-risk options, you'll probably look at

---

Reading and Study Tips

Abbreviations
Abbreviations are shortened words or series of initials used to represent titles or phrases. For example, ASAP is an abbreviation for "As Soon As Possible." Look for abbreviations in this section. On a separate sheet of paper, write five commonly used abbreviations.

" *Don't let the future be that time when you wish you'd done what you aren't doing now.* "

John Mason
Author

money market and stable asset funds, such as certificates of deposit, treasury bills and notes, and government and other fixed-income securities.

Contribution Plans

defined contribution plan a plan that pays benefits based on the amount in the employee's account plus any investment earnings

One way to save for your retirement is to participate in a defined contribution plan. **Defined contribution plans** pay benefits based on the amount in the employee's account plus any investment earnings. The employer usually makes a fixed-percentage contribution. For example, an employer may match your contribution dollar for dollar up to a certain percent.

These plans do not guarantee a fixed benefit amount. What you eventually receive will be determined by the ups and downs of the market. In many cases, you can choose where your money will be invested. If your company offers such a plan, make sure that you take an active role in how your money grows. Do your homework, keep a retirement portfolio, and make the system work for you.

Profit-Sharing   Employers can base their contributions on a percentage of your pay or on a percentage of the company's profits. In some plans, called discretionary profit-sharing plans, employers can decide from year to year whether they will contribute.

401(k)   A 401(k) plan, also known as a salary reduction plan, is often considered to be the best alternative to company pension plans. The company pays less for retirement benefits but usually matches part of your contribution. It is a way for you to set aside part of your salary before it is taxed; you can invest it and not have to pay any taxes on it until you retire. You have the freedom to choose your investments. You can make your own adjustments quarterly or daily, depending on your plan. If you change jobs, you can take your money with you. If you stay with the company, you can borrow against it. You pay no taxes on your account, the contributions you make, or your investment return until you either withdraw the funds or retire.

You better live your best and act your best and think your best today, for today is the sure preparation for tomorrow and all the other tomorrows that follow.

Harriet Martineau
English Author and Social Reformer

Simplified Employee Pensions (SEPs)   In simplified employee pension plans, the employer decides what percentage it will contribute to employee-owned accounts, which are invested by financial institutions, such as banks, credit unions, brokerage firms, insurance companies, or mutual fund companies.

Employee Stock Ownership Plans (ESOPs)   Employee stock ownership plans, or stock bonus plans, allow the employee to buy shares of company stock. The employer funds the plan with company stock or allows you to buy shares of stock as a plan investment option.

Health Care

Health care is a standard benefit that employers provide for their full-time employees. Most insurance plans are funded in part by the employee with the employer making some kind of contribution. Health care benefits also can include such things as maternity leave and sick leave.

Medical

Among the most popular medical insurance programs are point-of-service (POS) plans and health maintenance organizations (HMOs). Large companies often allow employees to choose between the two.

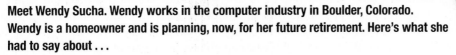

New Attitudes / New Opportunities

Meet Wendy Sucha. Wendy works in the computer industry in Boulder, Colorado. Wendy is a homeowner and is planning, now, for her future retirement. Here's what she had to say about . . .

Her financial goals and how she approached planning for her future. "At first I didn't really have any financial goals. I started off at the bottom rung of the pay scale and was on a tight budget. I knew that I needed to move into a department that had a better salary range. As I worked, more opportunities opened up, and the finances fell into place. Then I started planning. When you are used to making nothing and then you start getting some sizable checks, you definitely need to plan. That's when I analyzed what I wanted."

Looking into buying her first home. "I thought that a house wasn't actually possible. With one income, I needed a mortgage that was similar to my rent. My friend, a realtor, made the suggestion that I visit a mortgage specialist to see what I could afford and what was feasible at that point. It was very intimidating, but I knew that I had to move forward at some point. I was making good money and I was saving. I just needed to see how much I needed to save before I could actually pursue owning my own home.

"When I met with the mortgage banker, she looked at what I had made for the past two years and asked about my future financial goals. Still, I didn't really know how to proceed, so I took a course. It was offered by a not-for-profit organization that helps people under a salary range understand what they can afford and the different programs out there to help them. If you took this four-week course, you were eligible for a grant."

On making her plans happen and the advice she's relied on. "I learned by taking people's advice and researching it. I asked questions of all sorts of people and then further investigated some good suggestions. I found out that I should sell my stock and put some of it towards my new home and invest the rest of it. It was the most logical way to invest my money for my retirement and to save for the future.

"Some of the best advice I've received is: when you receive a paycheck, always pay yourself in a savings account. You never know what could happen, what the future holds. Besides, having an emergency fund is always a smart idea. I'm not a financial wizard, but it's not too hard to research what logical choices will help you save your money."

Point-of-Service Plans In POS plans, you choose a primary care physician (PCP). You can receive care through this individual or choose from any of the specialists in the network. Most plans cover a variety of preventative care, such as annual physicals, mammograms, and immunizations.

POS plans offer you the choice of receiving medical care from within a network of provider doctors and hospitals. These are individuals or institutions that have made an agreement with the company to provide services for its members. The benefits to the employee are greater if he or she chooses health care from within the network.

If the employee chooses to go to a doctor outside of the network of provider doctors and hospitals, the insurance company will cover a reduced percentage of the medical fees.

Health Maintenance Organizations HMO programs are less flexible. You choose one PCP to provide for routine and preventative care. But the PCP in HMOs is the only one who can refer you to a specialist. He or she coordinates all of your care and treatment. You must use hospitals and doctors within the network or else pay all of the cost. HMOs prize early detection and preventative care, so many preventative care procedures are fully covered.

Dental Plans Employers don't always provide dental coverage and, often, the employee must pay an additional amount to have it. Many companies provide a dental maintenance organization (DMO) dental plan that covers care given by dentists in a specific network. Other companies may be part of a group insurance plan that lets you choose your dentist, though in this case, coverage often is reduced.

DMOs usually cover 100 percent of preventative services, such as routine exams, cleanings, and X-rays. Some other services are fully covered, such as fillings and oral surgery. Other services, such as crowns and braces, are covered at a reduced rate.

Vision Vision care also is covered by network services. Vision service plans (VSPs) cover services and materials from doctors and eye care facilities in the network. Exams and eyeglass lenses are generally covered at 100 percent. Other materials, such as frames and contact lenses, are covered at a reduced rate.

Prescription Drugs Prescription drugs are generally included in medical coverage. You receive a card that you present to the pharmacist when you place your order. This card entitles you to a discount or requires you to make a small co-pay payment. A **co-pay payment** is a set amount the employee pays every time he or she buys prescriptions. Some companies offer mail order service for long-term prescriptions. Employees can get significant savings on medications they must have on a long-term daily basis.

co-pay payment a set amount the employee pays for health care or prescriptions, with the insurance company paying the remainder of the cost

Educational Savings

Soon, all 50 states and the District of Columbia will offer their residents the chance to invest in college savings plans. Called the 529 plan, this tax-free plan offers families a simple, safe, and affordable way to save for college. There are two options available. One is a prepaid tuition plan based on today's costs. This option guarantees to keep pace with tuition increases. The other option, a savings plan, provides families with a variable rate of return and does not guarantee to keep up with tuition increases. You can open an account with almost any amount and contribute small monthly payments, making the 529 plan affordable for most families.

> ❝ My interest is in the future because I am going to spend the rest of my life there. ❞
>
> *Charles F. Kettering*
> *Inventor and Electrical Engineer*

Having a Plan for after Work

You took the time to plan for your career and it paid off. Because you had a plan, you were better able to make informed decisions. Informed decisions can make your retirement successful as well.

Earlier, you learned about some of the options available for saving for retirement. Making a plan for your retirement will help you prepare for the future. Here are some additional questions you'll want to ask yourself before drafting your plan. Don't forget to include your significant other and your family in your plans.

- Do I even want to retire?
- Might I want to start another career?
- Will I ever want to own or start my own business?
- Where do I want to live? Do I want to start over in a new place?
- Do I want to maintain my current lifestyle?

You'll want to think about others things such as health care, estate planning, funeral expenses, insurance, and long-term nursing care. Take the time to write out

Figure 3.7 *Gail's Retirement Plan*

Lifestyle/Expenses

- Maintain current (debt-free) house to stay near children, grandchildren, and rental properties and keep position on hospital board of directors.
- Purchase rental properties–pay off debt within five years.
- Purchase condo in Arizona for winter months
- Play golf year round–golf club membership at home and in Arizona.
- Both will volunteer one year teaching business courses in African village career school.
- Take Alaskan and world cruises. Misc.
- Estate planning complete.
- Purchased retirement health care plan that includes long-term care and life insurance.
- Funerals have been planned and expenses paid.
- Continue paying into grandchildren's 529 college savings plans.

Finances/Income

- Arthur's 401(k)
- Gail's 401(k), teaching and hospital pensions
- Joint stock portfolio
- Sale of business
- Rental properties
- Social Security
- Board of Directors' salary

Thinking Critically Gail listed their goals, plans, and dreams for their retirement. *Have Gail and Arthur planned for a successful retirement? Why? Why not?*

your plan. For an example, look at Gail's retirement plan in Figure 3.7. Gail's home health care consulting firm has grown. She maintains a home office in a downtown office building and has two more branch locations in the suburbs. A young woman Gail mentored has offered to buy her business for a considerable sum. Because Gail and her husband, Arthur, want to stay active, they plan to live in semiretirement. Arthur is planning to retire from his career as a senior chemist. He will help Gail with the rental properties they plan to purchase.

QUICK RECAP 3.5

WORKING TO LIVE VERSUS LIVING TO WORK: PLANNING FOR THE LONG RUN

Now you should have a better idea of the benefits and importance of making long-range plans. Here is a quick summary:
- Most companies provide retirement and medical benefits to their full-time employees.
- Most companies help provide for the retirement of their employees.
- Most health care plans are funded in part by the employee, with the employer making some kind of contribution.

- The 529 savings plan is a tax-free, simple, safe, and affordable way for families to save for college.
- Making a plan is the key to a successful retirement.

CHECK YOURSELF

1. Name three defined contribution plans.
2. Name the two options available with the 529 college savings plan.

Check your answers online at **www.mhhe.com/pace.**

BUSINESS VOCABULARY

co-pay payment   a set amount the employee pays for health care or prescriptions, with the insurance company paying the remainder of the cost

defined contribution plan   a plan that pays benefits based on the amount in the employee's account plus any investment earnings

Chapter Summary

Section 3.1 Creating a Professional Reputation

Objective: *Define your morals and values.*

You learned that your reputation is the most important thing you have and that guarding it is your responsibility. You learned that values are the beliefs that govern your behavior and morals are standards upon which you judge what is good or bad and right or wrong. You discovered that ethics are the rules of conduct followed by a group or culture. You learned that the reputation of a company relies on the people who work for it.

Section 3.2 Building and Maintaining a Professional Network

Objective: *Build and maintain your professional network.*

You learned that a professional network consists of people outside of your office and with whom you do business. You discovered that burning bridges, backstabbing, and bad-mouthing can damage your reputation and your career.

Section 3.3 Professional Pride: Taking and Giving Credit and Recognition

Objective: *Explain why working in a team can be rewarding.*

You discovered that carefully handled self-promotion is good for your career. You learned about the rewards of working and taking credit as part of a team. You learned that your professional profile is a combination of your success, your reputation, your network, your résumé, and your portfolio.

Section 3.4 Using Your Experience

Objective: *Define what a mentor is and does.*

You learned that a mentor is a person who gives advice to others and helps them learn and grow to their fullest potential. You learned that to use your power responsibly, you need to stay away from unethical behavior and spend time doing community service or charity work. You discovered that in order to keep your career from stalling, you need to stay diverse and continue learning.

Section 3.5 Working to Live versus Living to Work: Planning for the Long Run

Objective: *Extend your goals into the future.*

You learned that planning for your retirement is just as important as planning for your career. You discovered that Social Security and company pensions are potentially unreliable. You learned that health care is a standard benefit that most employers provide for their full-time employees. You found that all 50 states and the District of Columbia offer residents the chance to invest in college savings plans. You learned that planning for retirement helps you make informed decisions.

Business Vocabulary

- code of ethics (p. 83)
- collaboration (p. 93)
- co-pay payment (p. 104)
- credentials (p. 84)
- database system (p. 89)
- defined contribution plans (p. 102)
- entrepreneurs (p. 100)

- ethics (p. 83)
- mentor (p. 97)
- mission statement (p. 90)
- morals (p. 82)
- motivation (p. 93)
- values (p. 82)
- visibility (p. 93)

Key Concept Review

1. Explain how treating others with respect and dignity helps you reach your career goals. (3.1)

2. How are your skills, credentials, and experience related to your reputation? (3.1)

3. Why are loyalty and personal commitment important for successful professionals? (3.2)

4. Explain the differences between your in-house network and your professional network. (3.2)

5. Describe what happens when teams collaborate and motivation is high. (3.3)

6. Explain the values teams need to have in today's workplace. (3.3)

7. Explain why many companies have their own mentoring programs. (3.4)

8. How is being a good boss similar to being a good mentor? (3.4)

9. What are the differences between POS and HMO health care plans? (3.5)

10. Explain why it is important to plan for retirement? (3.5)

Online Project

Joining a Professional Association

Research professional association Web sites for your chosen career or field. Find the criteria or cost for joining the group, and the time commitment involved, by downloading membership applications or visiting Web sites. Decide whether membership in the organizations would be a good networking tool. If so, take steps to join them.

Step Up the Pace

CASE A   *New Mentor*

You have been working for the same company for five years. You started at an entry-level position and have worked your way up to a position in management. You have been assigned an intern who will spend a month observing you in order to learn your side of the business. You know your job and business inside and out but are not sure how to explain what you know to your intern.

What to Do

1. Make a list of the 10 most important things you learned about your job and business over the past five years.
2. Think of instructive exercises, tours, or tasks that you can assign to your intern.

CASE B *Money Matters*

You have decided that you want to take control of your financial future. You have a steady income and a good job. You want to start saving for college, a house, and retirement, but you don't know what your options are.

What to Do

1. Think of your most immediate financial goals, your long-term goals, and your retirement goals. What do you want?
2. Research financial resources and advisors you might consult. Create a list of questions you want answered in order to help them understand your goals.

How to Calculate a Tip

When hosting a business lunch, you don't want to be embarrassed by leaving too little—or too much—of a tip. The current standard for tipping is to give the wait staff 15 to 20 percent of the total bill. Use these mental math tips to figure out how much you should leave.

Ten percent of anything is fairly easy to compute. Simply move the decimal one place to the left. For example, 10 percent of $25.00 is $2.50.

To find 20 percent, find 10 percent and then double it. So, 20 percent of $25.00 is $5.00.

To find 15 percent of a number, find 10 percent, then add on half of the answer. So, 15 percent of $25 is $3.75 ($2.50 + $1.25). Usually, it's easiest to round up.

Of course, your bill may not be as "neat" of a figure as $25. Round the bill to the nearest $5 or $10 range and calculate the tip using that rounded number.

One more tip about tipping: Never leave pennies. That is considered an insult.

Which tip amount is correct for a $53.50 restaurant bill?
A) $5.00   B) $5.50   C) $8.25   D) $10.00   E) $11.00

Choice C is about 15 percent and choice D is about 20 percent, so answers C, D, and E are correct.

Exercise: Fill in the chart to find the correct tip.

Bill Amount	Round to	10%	15%	20%
$19.34	$20.00	$2.00		
$72.65				
$35.80				
$59.20				
$43.02				
$32.55				
$114.00				

401K a retirement plan to which both the employee and employer contribute

A

abstract services read the latest books and articles and give a summary of the content

aggressive expressing one's rights at the expense of the rights of others

assertive expressing yourself and your rights without infringing on the rights of others

B

behavioral interview uses a line of questioning that seeks to find out how you reacted in the past

benchmarks measurable steps that help you meet your goals

C

chronological résumé lists education and experiences with the most recent listed first

code of ethics written rules of conduct for the members of a group or organization to follow

collaboration working together

combination résumé emphasizes skills and education as well as work experience

committee interview one person is interviewed by a group of people

complacent satisfied with things as they are

co-pay payment a set amount the employee pays for health care or prescriptions, with the insurance company paying the remainder of the cost

cost-of-living statistics statistics based on the price people in an area pay for products and services, such as housing, food, utilities, and transportation

credentials education and professional knowledge gained, such as degrees and certificates

cross-trained trained on another job

D

database system a computer program that stores all like information in the same place

defined contribution plan a plans that pays benefits based on the amount in the employee's account plus any investment earnings

discussion groups also called *Usenet;* public online groups where you can discuss a topic

downsize cuts to a workforce because of financial difficulties

E

electronic résumé used when posting online or sending via e-mail; and contains no formatting

entrepreneurs people who start their own businesses

ethics rules of conduct followed by a group or culture

F

functional résumé emphasizes education and training over experience

G

goal something you put effort into achieving

group interview several job hopefuls are interviewed by one to or two interviewers at one time

I

informational interview a way for you to get information about your career from someone already in the field

J

job description a summary of the position and its responsibilities

L

lateral move a move from one position in a department to a similar position in another department

M

mailing lists also called *listservs;* private or public group e-mail discussions

mentor a person who gives advice to others and helps them learn and grow to their fullest potential

mission statement a written statement of a company's purpose, business, and values

morals standards upon which one judges what is good or bad, right and or wrong

motivation the will to act

multitasking doing more than one thing at a time

N

nepotism favoritism shown toward family members when granting jobs

network people you know and with whom you can share valued information

O

one-to-one interview a prospective employee is interviewed by only one person

online courses also called *virtual college;* university/college-level distance learning courses offered online

P

portfolio an organized example of the work you have done in your career

prioritize to order a task according to each respective task's relative importance

promotion a boost in position or job title

R

resignation a formal notification of departure from a company

S

screening interview a chance for the employer to see if you have the skills and qualifications for the job

situational interview similar to a behavioral interview, except you are asked to describe how you would handle a situation

stress interview uses a line of stressful questioning so the employer can evaluate how the interviewee handles stress

T

telecommuting employees work at home part or all of the week instead of working at the office

teleworking employees use telecommunications technology to work anywhere away from the office

U

unstructured interview the interviewer asks one or two broad questions

V

values the beliefs that prompt one's behavior

visibility involves doing good work and letting others know about it

Photo Credits

3: © Myrleen Ferguson/PhotoEdit; **43:** © David Young-Wolff/PhotoEdit; **81:** © Adrian Peacock/Creatas

I

J

K

L

M

N

O

P